# CURRICULUM PLANNING IN GEOGRAPHY

# CURRICULUM PLANNING
# IN
# GEOGRAPHY

## Norman J. Graves

*Professor of Education,*
*University of London Institute*
*of Education*

HEINEMANN EDUCATIONAL BOOKS

Heinemann Educational Books Ltd
LONDON  EDINBURGH  MELBOURNE  AUCKLAND  TORONTO
KINGSTON  HONG KONG  SINGAPORE  KUALA LUMPUR
IBADAN  NAIROBI  JOHANNESBURG
LUSAKA  NEW DELHI


British Library CIP Data

Graves, Norman John
    Curriculum planning in geography
    1. Geography— Study and teaching (Secondary)— Great Britain
    2. Curriculum planning — Great Britain
    I. Title
    910'.7'1241          G74


ISBN 0−435−35313−6
ISBN 0−435−35312−8 Pbk


© Norman J. Graves 1979
First published 1979


Published by
Heinemann Educational Books Ltd
48 Charles Street, London W1X 8AH
Printed in Great Britain by Richard Clay (The Chaucer Press) Ltd,
Bungay, Suffolk

# Contents

475032

# Preface

Since the conceptual revolution in geography teachers have been hard pressed not only to keep up to date with geography, but also to develop their own curricula. The problem of curriculum planning is one which is dependent on curriculum theory on the one hand and on geographical theory on the other. This book is a first modest attempt to bring these two theoretical realms explicitly together with a view to helping geography teachers to plan their courses.

In the past syllabus planning has been much influenced by the traditional frameworks used, be these regional, systematic or concentric, and the emphasis was on the content to be taught, this being an admixture of facts and principles. The syllabus tended to be seen as stable not to say static over many years. Today we are much more conscious of the need to understand the curriculum process as a dynamic system tending to modify what is taught owing to the changing elements within the system, be these educational objectives, subject content or teaching strategies. It is with this interactive view of the geography curriculum that this book is concerned.

For the book's imperfections, I alone am responsible. I should nevertheless like to thank Michael Williams of Manchester University and Joseph Stoltman of Western Michigan University who gave critical readings to the manuscript and made many helpful suggestions. To Alice Henfield I am thankful for she attempted to make typographical sense of my handwriting.

Norman J. Graves

April 1978

# Acknowledgements

The author and the publishers are grateful to the following authors and their publishers for allowing the text or illustrative material indicated to be reproduced in this book:

D. Cromarty and the Geographical Association, Figure 4.3, from *Teaching Geography*, Vol. 1, No. 1, 1975, p 29; East Midlands Regional Examination Board, Chapter 7 Appendix B, from Syllabus of CSE Mode 3 Shared Scheme in Geography Based on the Geography for the Young School Leaver Project; Michael Eraut, Len Goad and George Smith, and the University of Sussex Education Area, Chapter 7 Appendix C, from *The Analysis of Curriculum Materials*, 1975; Kemp and Fearon Publishers, Figure 2.4(b), from *Kemp's Book of Instructional Design*, 1971; J. F. Kerr and Hodder and Stoughton, Figure 1.3, from *Changing the Curriculum*, 1968; Michael Walker and the Geographical Association, Figure 4.1, from *Teaching Geography*, Vol. 1, No. 4, 1976, pp 163−4.

# Acknowledgements

The author and the publishers are grateful to the following for permission to reproduce copyright material.

# CHAPTER ONE

# The Nature of the Problem

**Introduction**

Essentially a teacher's curriculum problem would seem that of deciding (1) *what* he is going to try to get his students to learn; (2) *how* he is going to manage this operation of making them learn what he has decided is worthwhile; and (3) how he is going to evaluate what has in fact happened in the learning process so that he can act in an appropriate manner next time round. Put this way, the problem seems clear, even if the operation of getting students to learn something worthwhile may in practice be a difficult one. In the context of geography, I might decide that I wish to teach a class of 15-year-old students that there is a regularity about the spacing of settlements and that there are economic and technical reasons for this. I might attempt to do this by getting them first to measure the distance between certain towns on a topographical map and then refer them to field investigations on the field of influence of a market town before discussing the concept of the breaking point between two fields of influence of nearby towns (Davies 1976). I might evaluate the whole activity by noting the students' reactions in class (were they reasonably interested?), by examining their course work and by checking that in their answers to a short test on the concepts discussed, 75 per cent of the students gained more than, say, half marks.

So what is the problem? It seems clear that if what I have written describes fairly accurately what has happened in the past or what may happen in the future, then the teacher's curriculum problem appears to resolve itself to finding suitable objectives, arranging appropriate learning experiences for the students and to finding ways of evaluating these learning experiences. It all seems relatively simple.

Alas it is all too deceptively simple. For how does the teacher choose his objectives? Are they to be short-term, perhaps behavioural objectives or more distant long-term aims? How does my teaching about the spacing of settlements fit into the total geography curriculum, let alone how does it fit into the whole school curriculum? What criteria should I use to choose short-term objectives and what values do I assume when I do so? Is it really possible to base a geography curriculum on a series of short-term objectives or is this crying for the moon? What is the relationship between the way I arrange learning experiences for the students and my objectives? How does my teaching style fit into this or is it irrelevant? What difference do the resources at my command make to the ultimate learning which takes place? Can I really evaluate the unintended learning as well as what I hoped would be learned? Can I really evaluate the classroom process myself, or do I need someone from outside to help me? If I do need someone from outside, who is there to call upon and what exactly should I ask him to do? How do I act upon receipt of an evaluation report on a curriculum which I have designed? What credence should I attach to it? How far should I be influenced by curriculum developers who may be operating in another school in a different context? Is there a handy instrument which I could use to help me plan my geography curriculum?

The purpose of this book is to try to examine some of these questions and to suggest some answers in the context of geography. It should be clear that since the present education system is in a dynamic state, no answers suggested can be definitive. They will all be provisional and based on our present knowledge of the curriculum process. Let us first look briefly at the evolution of the problem.

**Curriculum planning in geography: historical perspectives**
It is useful in order to understand the present situation to look briefly at what has happened in the past. First it must be understood that not only have ideas about curriculum planning changed, but so has the terminology, the whole context of schooling and the subject of geography. It would therefore be absurd to expect a discussion on curriculum planning in geography in 1980 to sound the same as one did in 1880. Yet it is surprising how far our own thinking is shaped by formative experiences we had years ago, perhaps when we were at University or at a College of Education or even when we were pupils

at school. For example, the term 'curriculum' has evolved considerably in meaning over the past 50 years and it will no doubt go on to change its meaning as the social situation in which it is used also changes. Yet many of us go on ascribing a meaning to the term which is now no longer relevant. Further it has to be accepted that even at a given point in time, different people (or even the same person at different times) will use the word in two or more different senses. Confusion can be seen to arise rather early in such circumstances.

The traditional conception of curriculum planning in geography may be exemplified by reference to suggestions contained in the literature on geographical education of the nineteenth century and of the first 50 years of the twentieth century. In essence the process was as follows.

First, a decision was taken by the headteacher or by an official or a Committee that geography was worth including in the school curriculum. (Here the word curriculum means the totality of the content of education that the school offers to its students: mathematics, English, history, geography, physical education, games etc.)

Secondly, the teacher in charge of geography (or a suitable official body where the education system is centralized) drew up a 'syllabus'. A syllabus was essentially a list of content deemed appropriate for the students and derived from the totality of what the subject had to offer. Thus parts of the syllabus for a secondary school might have read:

*Year 2*
Southern continents
Lowlands − Amazon and Congo Basins
Highlands − Northern Andes and East Africa
Tropical Regions − Queensland and Brazil
Deserts − the Nile Valley and the Atacama
Subtropical Regions − North-west Africa, Central Chile, South-
west and South-east Australia.                    (IAAM 1967)

Thirdly, the teacher actually teaching particular groups of students would draw up a series of 'lesson plans' which would indicate how he intended to teach the content outlined in the syllabus. At this stage, objectives might appear since the teacher might reasonably be expected to have a clear idea of what he was attempting to achieve.

Such a lesson plan used with a class of 12−13-year-olds is reproduced below. It is part of a group of lessons or 'teaching unit' on the Amazon Basin whose general objectives were:

1. to reinforce the skills of searching for relevant information, including atlas map reading, graphic skills and report writing;
2. to teach the concept of mean temperature range and rainfall régime;
3. to show at an elementary level that the tropical rain forest forms an ecosystem;
4. to demonstrate the difficulties of exploiting such a forest.

The topic of the first 'lesson' was the tropical or equatorial rain forest. The plan is set out in the form used by the teacher.

## SPECIFIC OBJECTIVES

1. To locate the Selvas in South America.
2. To describe the nature of the forest: its flora and fauna.

## THE MATERIALS AND EQUIPMENT

1. An outline map of South America showing:
   (a) the extent of the Selvas;
   (b) an inset map showing the flight of airplane which crashed in the forest (Figure 1.1) (one for each student).
2. An account of air crash in the forest by a survivor (to be read by the teacher).
3. An overhead projector transparency of a drawing of a typical section of the equatorial forest and a photocopy of the same drawing (Figure 1.2) (one for each student).
4. A textbook picture of the equatorial forest (each student had one).

## PROCEDURE

1. Give out maps and drawings.
2. Examine aerial photograph of Amazon forest in the textbook and ask for descriptions.
3. Locate approximate spot where photograph was taken on Atlas map of South America.
4. Students to shade in area of forest on the outline map of South America provided and measure its East-West and North-South extent in kilometres.
5. Relate the incident of Juliane Koepcke who was travelling by air from Lima to Pucallpa (See Figure 1.1 inset), and read the following passage:

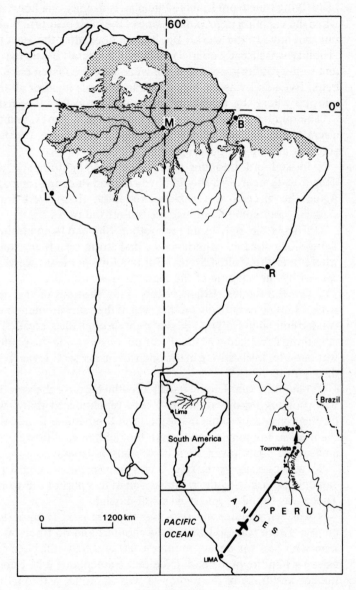

FIGURE 1.1

'The flying time from Lima to Pucallpa is usually one hour, and when the visibility is good this is one of the most beautiful flights one can have in the world. But half an hour after the start the visibility was already poor. Then later the aircraft began to roll, and as the rolling grew worse we were asked to fasten our seat belts. Even so I was not afraid. Air turbulence is, after all, not unusual where the mountains curve down towards the east.

'The rain began pattering against the window panes, and the aircraft was thrown about vertically. There were the first screams among the passengers.

'I looked out into the clouds and saw lightning; it was dangerously near. We should have reached Pucallpa long ago. Again the aircraft was rocking violently, there were more screams, and some hand luggage fell off the racks.

' "This is the end," said my mother. She had been afraid of flying since she had experienced a bad storm on a flight somewhere over the United States. But this time her fears were not caused by the shaking of the plane – it was on fire.

'I saw the flames. Bright yellow, they shot out of the right wing. I looked over to my mother, but at the same moment there was a tremendous jolt that passed right through the aircraft. The next thing I realized was that I was no longer inside the plane. I was outside. I was sitting in the open air on my seat. I was flying through the air.

'I remember that I could hardly breathe because the seat belt was pressing on my stomach. I also remembered that I was turning round and round in the air. And I remember finally that the trees in the jungle underneath looked like cauliflower, lots and lots of cauliflower, then I lost consciousness.

'I was woken up by the rain. It was pouring down as hard as it can only pour during the rainy season in this part of the world. There was thunder, and it was still daylight.

'I was lying under my seat, but the seat next to mine was empty. There was no trace of my mother, and no trace of the man who had sat on my mother's left and had still been fast asleep when the plane had made that tremendous jolt. I could not see any trace of the plane – I was all alone, with only the croaking of frogs and the chirping of insects.'

(from *The Observer Colour Supplement*)

6. Ask the class to write down a few ideas of what they would have

done if they had found themselves in the same situation.

7. Compare these suggestions with what Juliane Koepcke actually did (Found a river and followed it).

8. Ask for suggestions as to why this was a sensible thing to do.

9. Show drawing of structure of Tropical rain forest and ask students to label each part after discussion of what drawing shows (Figure 1.2).

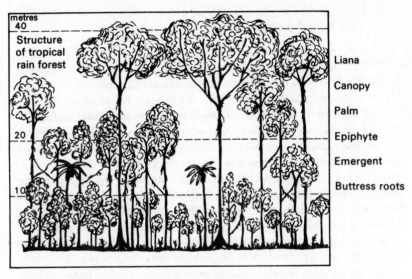

FIGURE 1.2

10. Juliane Koepcke eventually found a hut and wood cutters who brought her out of the jungle. Ask class to find out from following passage what had troubled her most in the forest.

'For the first time in nine nights I had a roof over my head. But I slept badly. The mosquitoes tortured me. I kept listening through the night for the sound of human voices, but this was a stupid thing to hope for because nobody ever travelled in the jungle at night.

'The maggots were causing me terrible pain and I kept hearing things in the jungle. Sometimes I would hear a monkey scream, or a parrot, and sometimes I thought I heard dangerous animals moving in the undergrowth. But, despite everything, I dozed and finally went to sleep.

'The next morning I found a tube of Vaseline in the hut and rubbed it on myself in the hope of getting rid of the maggots, but it was no use. So I tried to make a skewer out of a piece of palm branch to dig the maggots out. I dug out twenty-five of them in this way and then picked out some more with my teeth.

'My right arm was getting worse and again I began to worry that it would have to be amputated if I did not get help soon ...'

11. Try to obtain suggestions to why the insects are more troublesome than the bigger animals of the jungle.


The teacher could read advice on how best to structure his lessons in the literature on teaching methods. He could also find out about visual and other teaching aids. Thus the lesson plan might be more or less influenced by the teacher's predilection on 'methods' and teaching aids as well as by what he considered to be valuable objectives.

Fourthly, the teacher would evaluate student learning (and therefore by implication his teaching) by giving class tests and by school and public examinations. The concept of feedback was accepted but generally limited to that affecting methods – that is if something had not been grasped by the student, then there might be a case for changing the method, not so much the content or the objectives.

Given that geography teaching in Great Britain became a normal part of the secondary school curriculum in the twentieth century, the important aspects of curriculum planning were syllabus construction, lesson construction and testing or examinations. Indeed most books on the teaching of geography devote space to these topics. Fairgrieve (1926) who dominated the world of geographical education in Great Britain for many years launched the idea that a geography syllabus 'must cover the world. Otherwise what is taught is not Geography'. Various authorities have re-echoed Fairgrieve including Long and Roberson (1966) and, although he is less forthright about it, Bailey (1974) seems to favour such syllabuses since he writes 'Geography is the only subject in the curriculum which by its nature tells pupils what places and peoples are like. This surely is essential information for the informed citizen, the conveying of which is an important objective of any course in geography. Region-based courses, or at least, courses which include substantial elements of regional description and analysis, probably do this most effectively'. Although regional syllabuses were not the only ones in vogue (systematic and concentric syllabuses were launched in the 1950s (Briault and Shave 1952) evidence is strong that right up to the late 1960s, much curriculum planning in geography was based on a regional syllabus framework (Hogan 1962, Graves 1968). This was associated with what was then the commonly accepted research paradigm in geography, namely the 'areal differentiation' or 'regional synthesis' paradigm.

In consequence teachers tended to exercise their ingenuity in finding suitable means of teaching skills, ideas and values within a framework of regions. Thus one might attempt to show that architecture may be influenced by climate in the context of Greece or Italy, that heavy industry developed on coalfields in the context of Britain or Germany, that extensive farming was a function of the ratio of land area to labour force in the context of North America, that the evidence for glacial erosion processes could be seen and studied in the context of the Alps or the Western Cordillera. This system of syllabus construction was sometimes called 'planned incidentalism' because it was deliberately planned that each region studied would be used to teach what incidentally that region most adequately revealed. A major drawback to this system was that in application it often degenerated to a mere description of each region covered.

With the advent of the 'conceptual revolution' in geography which in Great Britain may be dated as beginning in schools from 1965 with the publication of *Frontiers in Geographical Teaching*, (Chorley, Hagget 1965), some geographers began to question more and more the assumptions that curriculum planning in geography could be based on a regional framework. In the first place the 'areal differentiation' paradigm of geography was no longer widely accepted as one representing the kind of research currently being undertaken in geography, hence there appeared to be a disjunction between what schools were doing and what professional geographers were doing. That this disjunction is valid and reasonable has become a source of debate in school geography departments. In the second place the whole conception of curriculum and curriculum planning had undergone a considerable change owing to research work undertaken in the U.S.A., Sweden and lately in the U.K., and the idea that a syllabus was the linchpin of curriculum planning began to be questioned. Let us briefly examine the evolution of these ideas.

First it is important to understand that part of the confusion which sometimes occurs in relation to the term curriculum arises because some writers conceive the curriculum as what actually happens in a school and others as what is planned for the school. The first conception is essentially descriptive and analytical and relates to what experiences the students and teachers have had, what they learn from these and how the whole process actually works. Thus it comprises not only the formal curriculum, i.e. the activities which are time-tabled (e.g. map reading on the Scarborough sheet of the 1 : 50 000 topographical map for Class 4B so that they can learn to distinguish between land forms on the Wolds, Vale of Pickering and North York Moors) but also the so called 'hidden curriculum' that is what they *also* learn even though there may be no overt intention that they should learn this. For example they may learn, that if they want to please their geography teacher then they had better not argue with him on whether an interpretation he gives of a road pattern is valid or not from the map evidence, because he, does not take kindly to having his authority questioned. The second conception is really a normative one, that is, it describes what ought to happen in a school or what is planned to happen, not what necessarily will happen. Clearly, unless every activity in the school is entirely spontaneous, then the curriculum is bound to be planned to some extent, so that curriculum planning is clearly a legitimate and useful activity, but it is not the same activity as what actually happens when an attempt is made to put the plan into operation. For one thing, in most schools a geography curriculum plan has to be put into operation by different teachers and this in itself will be sufficient to ensure that the actual curriculum will be different, at least in some significant way, from the planned curriculum. One teacher I taught with decided to start at one end of a regional syllabus while I started at the other!

The second important aspect of the curriculum is that for a long time, it was conceived of as a body of skills and knowledge to be learnt by the pupils and students. Although there were disagreements about what those skills and knowledge should be, there was general agreement that a curriculum was a conglomerate of courses of study to be assimilated in school, or to put it another way a curriculum was the content of education. Indeed most of the nineteenth century official reports on education spelled out in some detail what ought to be taught in various kinds of schools and a twentieth century book on the curriculum was called 'An essay on the content of education' (James 1949). Now this may sound commonsensical, but gradually we have come to think of curriculum not as a content to be taught and absorbed but as a process taking place in a teaching-learning system

(Wheeler 1967). In other words we look upon the curriculum as something dynamic and the content of a subject or discipline as one element in the system.

This is easily illustrated by reference to the geography curriculum. A teacher may have in mind that his students should learn to understand how various functional zones in towns come to be established. To bring this about he may provide them with fieldwork experiences which make them aware that such zones exist in reality; with documentary evidence of how such zoning has evolved over time and with data about rents and incomes in various zones of the town. But to get the students thinking about the concepts and processes involved the teacher will probably pose questions about the information provided and set exercises for the students. The students may discuss among themselves some of the ideas suggested by the teacher and by the documentary evidence, and they may put queries to the teacher. Thus the ideas and skills that the students may learn are the content element in the curriculum process; other elements are: the objectives of the teacher, the teaching strategy that he employs, the resources he provides and the students' behaviour, which itself is dependent on their own objectives and perceptions of that what the teacher is about. This view of the curriculum is summarized by Tanner and Tanner (1975) as 'Curriculum as experience'.

The outcome of such views of the curriculum as an interactive process has been the development of various models of how the curriculum process works, starting with the simple linear model put forward by Tyler (1949) and subsequently modified, elaborated and transformed by Taba (1962), Wheeler (1967), Kerr (1968), Lawton (1973) and many others. Most of these are general models of the curriculum, that is they purport to give the teacher a picture of how a school curriculum as a whole may work. For example Kerr's model is represented diagramatically in Figure 1.3.

It shows that the curriculum process consists of the interaction of a series of influences consisting of (1) educational objectives derived from various sources; (2) the disciplines of knowledge from which teachers may select; (3) school learning experiences which are themselves influenced by many factors; and (4) evaluation procedures. Now such a model is useful in clarifying the workings of the whole curriculum process. Every teacher whether he subscribes to this model or not, must base his actions on a perceived model of how the curriculum process works otherwise he would be unable to do any-

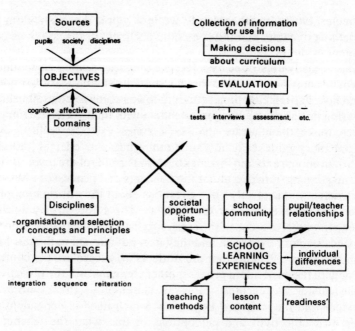

FIGURE 1.3. A model for curriculum theory.

thing. But most teachers are not in the position of having to develop a grand design for the whole school curriculum; they are responsible for certain aspects of the curriculum and geography teachers in particular are responsible for the geography curriculum only, even if they cooperate in teams on combined subject curricula. The trouble with many books on the curriculum is that they deal with the topic in a very general way and seldom in a manner which gives specific guidance to the subject teacher. Further, many are concerned with philosophical issues rather than with immediate practical problems. For example Hugh Sockett (1976) begins a book entitled *Designing the Curriculum* by writing, 'This is not a book on how to design a curriculum', which might prompt one to suggest that the book is mis-titled. He does go on to explain, 'It [the book] is concerned with philosophical issues in such design', which is undoubtedly intellectually stimulating, but the need to apply such studies to the practical tasks of curriculum planning remains.

It may be useful at this stage to summarize what we have found out about the use of the word *curriculum* in order to be clear about its various meanings. In the first place it is used in a very general sense to indicate the broad scope of the activities which go on in a school. In this sense it is not very precise; it merely shows that within a school certain types of learning may be expected to occur, for example within the area of English language, of mathematics, of physical education, of natural science, etc. In the second place, it may be used to indicate the content of a particular subject or area of knowledge which is to be taught. In the U.K. the word syllabus was often used to denote this content aspect of curriculum. Content refers to the ideas, concepts, principles, facts and skills which may be taught. In the third place, the term curriculum is used to indicate the process whereby aims, objectives, content, teaching strategies, and evaluation interact in the school; this is the dynamic aspect of the curriculum in action. In the fourth place, the term curriculum may be used to describe what is planned to happen in a school within a particular subject area. For example, the geography curriculum could be set out in a document which shows clearly what the aims of a course are, what the content consists of, what teaching units, with their objectives and teaching strategies are to be used, and how the course is to be evaluated. This could be called the *planned geography curriculum*. Clearly such a planned geography curriculum can only be well conceived if the planners understand the nature of the curriculum process.

Apart from model syllabuses which may be found in a number of texts on geographical education (Long 1964, Long and Roberson 1966, Graves 1971) there has been a paucity of advice on how to apply the broad findings from curriculum planning to geography. This is not surprising since the concept of curriculum planning has only recently begun to emerge, even though Tyler's seminal work was published in 1949 and was based on ideas he developed in the 1930s and early 1940s. Even in the United States of America where most of the curriculum research was born, the application of curriculum planning to geography did not really develop until the late 1960s. It is true that in 1963 the National Council for Geographic Education (a body roughly equivalent to the Geographical Association in the U.K.) published a book entitled Curriculum Guide for Geographic Education (Hill 1963), and in the preface the editor wrote, 'The intent of this volume is to present guidelines for geographic education for the assistance of those concerned with curriculum development in the Unites States.... It is hoped that the materials will be especially helpful to directors of curriculum and instruction, supervisors, principals, teachers, professors, and others who work on curriculum committees.' But although the book has useful chapters on the major concepts of geography, on geographic skills and techniques, on the evaluation of geographic learning, on resources for geographic education, what might have been the most useful chapter of all, namely one on suggested sequences for geographic learning turns out to contain a fairly traditional syllabus in which the secondary school course (grades 6 to 12 inclusive) is effectively based on regions or world divisions. Only in grades 10–12 (senior high school 15–18-year-olds) are there alternative courses suggested in physical geography, elementary meteorology and in conservation or resource management. However, it is a seminal book for curriculum planning in geography because it clearly recognised that such planning was not just a matter of putting a syllabus together and using appropriate teaching methods. But it made no mention of the curriculum process and it seems quite clear that the various authors were not generally aware of what their colleagues were doing in the field of curriculum theory and had had little experience of curriculum development projects.

By the time *The New Social Studies in Secondary Schools* (Fenton 1966) was published, both the editor and several of the authors had become involved in curriculum development projects in the social studies field. The American High School Geography Project had been started in 1961 and experience of deliberate curriculum development in geography was being acquired. Thus the geographical contributions to Fenton's book reflect not only changes in geography but also experience of trying out in schools problem solving approaches to its teaching. What they also show is that the teachers who expound their experiments are more conscious of the curriculum process involving objectives derived from the subject and from the students, a teaching strategy emphasizing the research methodology of geography rather than its conclusions. But little was said about curriculum planning as such. The only significant contribution came from a social scientist (Oliver 1966) who suggested certain criteria for selecting content in the social sciences.

In 1969 there came out of Australia a significantly titled book, *Programme Planning in Geography* (Biddle & Shortle 1969). It was significant in the sense that it was the first book which was devoted entirely to the theory and practice of planning curricula in geography, albeit in the context of New South Wales. It consists of an admixture of chapters discussing the principles of planning particular programmes and examples of the ways such programmes were in fact planned in various schools in New South Wales. Because the syllabus was centrally determined, the book is mainly concerned with giving advice on the interpretation of the syllabus and its implementation. Although the overall aims of the syllabuses are considered in the planning strategy, it is possible to see the predominance of content on the implementation. For example a fourth-form programme for Cabramatta High School and devised by M. H. Barlow began as follows:

## 11.   INTRODUCTION

The course outlined − content, purpose. Books, routine, projects, etc. The concept of a 'shrinking world', the necessity for an informed electorate, the 'cold war' and other controversial issues: Western Europe.

1. Introduction: past and present role in world affairs − discoveries, industrial and agrarian revolutions, world wars, trade. Importance to Australia in particular − trade, Commonwealth, immigration, culture.
2. Political geography: maps of countries, main cities, and features of Europe. Groupings and alliances − Common Market, EFTA, NATO, main personalities and current events in Europe.
3. Physical build: main physical regions on map − Southern Peninsulas, Southern Mountains, Northern Plain, Northern Shield − revision of glaciation. Contrast between north and south. Main rivers.
4. . . . .

However, as one progresses up the school to the senior forms (17-year-olds) one begins to see a greater emphasis on objectives and learning experiences but not on evaluation as the latter is provided by the external examination. The same teacher (M. H. Barlow) sets out the aims of senior high school geography and part of his programme reads as shown in Figure 1.4.

One can detect a greater consciousness of the curriculum process, although no reference is made in the book to curriculum theory. Thus the book, though a great advance of what had existed prior to its publication, still belongs to the era before geographical education was

| Topic, Treatment, Time | Skills and Activities |
|---|---|
| **Introduction (¹/₂ week)** | |
| (a) *Outline of Course* (2 Lessons). Definition of geography—study of environmental relationships within a regional setting; content of geography. Parts of the course—the topics and timing in each; systematic and regional approaches to geography. | (a) Critical thinking—to discuss systematic and regional approaches. |
| (b) *Classroom Routine* (1 Lesson). The use of binders—advantages; demonstration. Use of geography room—equipment; emphasis on private research and experiments; system of assignments; use of library. | (b) Visit to geography room to see equipment; and to library. |
| **Section One–The Hydrologic Cycle** | |
| (a) *Importance* (1 Lesson). Role of *Water in Geographic Processes and Patterns*—e.g., in weather and climate, upon biotic response, on the land surface, and upon man and his activities (especially farming). Water Cycle as theme for Part A—reference ahead to relevant topics to show unifying effect; diagram of Water Cycle. | (a) Discussion—of the effects of recent droughts and floods on each aspect mentioned. Diagram—of the Cycle. |
| (b) *Operation of the Cycle* (6 Lessons). *Sequence of the Cycle*—use above diagram and illustrative statistics to explain evaporation and transpiration, condensation and precipitation, and infiltration and runoff; refer briefly to role of each phase of cycle in later topics (e.g., runoff and landforms, groundwater and agriculture). The *Energy Basis of the Cycle*—solar energy as the driving force; exchange of this energy as moisture changes its states during the cycle (i.e., latent energy); the heat balance between atmosphere, surface, and space (gross input = gross output). Emphasis in this work is to be on the water cycle as a continuous working mechanism with a powerful driving force. | (b) Diagram—more detailed diagrams of each phase of the Cycle. Research—reading of text and references on phases of the Cycle. Vocabulary—entry of new terms in personal 'dictionaries.' |
| *Groundwater in More Detail*—terminology such as 'water table,' 'artesian,' 'aquifier,' 'permeable,' 'porous,' etc; movement of groundwater and shape of water table; Australian artesian basins (size, qualities, uses, problems). | Mapping—draw map of Australian underground water resources. Research—into CSIRO material on Hunter Valley water resources and problems. |
| *A Sample Study*—details of precipitation, infiltration, runoff, evapotranspiration, etc. in the Hunter Valley to illustrate the cycle in a small area. | |
| *Illustrative 'Experiment'* (2 Lessons)—simple demonstration of groundwater in geography 'laboratory' using a fishtank, sand, and plasticine arranged into an aquifer-aquiclude model. Coloured water to be used to show artesian and sub-artesian flow. | Practical experiment—class to help plan, record and analyse the 'experiment.' |

FIGURE 1.4. Sample from physical geography programme for senior high school (M. H. Barlow).

fertilized by ideas from curriculum theory. This shows that there is an inevitable lag before ideas in one area of education are seen to have relevance in another area. This does not imply that teachers were not coping with the curriculum process, but that the curriculum theory was implicit rather than explicit.

In the U.K. it was not until experience of curriculum development began to be assimilated that the full complexity of the task of curriculum planning began to be appreciated, though Hilda Taba had warned about this in her Curriculum Development: Theory and Practice (1962). Geography teachers have been slow to latch on to curriculum theory, but it became evident in the papers which emanated from various curriculum development projects in the late 1960s and early 1970s that use was being made of curriculum theory. This was particularly true not only of the Geography 14–18 project team but also of the Geography for the Young School leaver and the History Geography Social Science 8–13 project teams. Thus when I wrote *Geography in Education* (1975) it was possible to include some consideration of the curriculum process in geographical education (chapter 6) based on curriculum theory and on curriculum development projects' experience. No attempt was made to hammer out any particular curriculum plan in geography, though the broad criteria for such a plan were indicated based on a model devised by Biddle (1974). Hall (1976) is also very conscious of the curriculum process, though he also eschews any detailed consideration of planning the geography curriculum except in giving an example of the A level syllabus prepared by the 'West Midlands Study Group'. Marsden (1976) also refers to the general curriculum process and spells out in detail the various elements involved, but he also seems not to subscribe to any particular planning model except for content (p. 256) and by implication when he suggests certain curriculum units. Bailey (1974) who has a chapter on 'Planning the Programme' in his *Teaching Geography* gives sound practical advice but seems not to use any overall curriculum theory in writing about programme planning.

Meanwhile the literature on the curriculum in general has gone on expanding. If one thinks only of the first five years of the 1970s, then, in the U.K., not only are there a large number of Schools' Council publications, but also numerous works by specialists like Lawton (1973, 1975, 1977), Owen (1973), Warwick (1975), Stenhouse (1975), Sockett (1976), MacDonald and Walker (1976), Hamilton (1976), Pring (1976), Reynolds and Skilbeck (1976), and Barrow (1976). As one teacher said to me in a seminar 'It's certainly a growth area, but I wonder whether it's any use'.

The comment by the teacher reflected his concern for ideas and skills which would have a pay-off in the practice of teaching. A teacher is influenced by many factors in society, but if one narrows down consideration to those factors emanating from the 'education industry' then it is possible to subdivide them into two groups: (a) those which influence his general understanding of the educational process and (b) those which influence him directly in teaching his subject matter. The literature on the curriculum in general relates to the first group of factors while the literature on the geography curriculum relates to the second. Both may be 'useful' in the ultimate analysis since how a teacher carries out his work is as much a product of his general understanding as his special teaching skills; but the literature on the geography curriculum addresses itself to the more immediate problems and in this particular instance to the problems of curriculum planning in geography.

## The curriculum problem in geography

The curriculum problem for the geography teacher can be seen to exist at several levels and in numerous dimensions.

First there is the question of how the total curriculum is to be planned in the secondary school.  This is a question which, in the United Kingdom, has been exercising many minds recently. As the 'Great Debate' on education has proceeded (D.E.S. 1977(a) ) ideas have been tossed about concerning the structure and content of the secondary school curriculum (D.E.S. 1977(b) ). Should there be a common curriculum content for all students or a common core with some choice of content outside the core? What should the content of the common curriculum or common core consist of? Should geography be a part of the common core because of its contribution to graphicacy? How far should the curriculum be concerned with vocational training and thereby contribute to the instrumental aims of education? Can geography be thought of as a subject contributing to vocational education? Is geography to be taught as a separate subject throughout, or is it to be part of a broader group of subjects in the first two or three years and then taught as a separate subject? Or should it be, as at the Thomas Bennett School Crawley, where the reverse is true and geography after existing as a separate subject is taught as part of a Humanities Faculty in the 4th and 5th years. In any case how does the geography taught relate to any other part of the curriculum?

Secondly there is the problem of deciding what kind of geography to teach. Clearly this is related not only to changes in geography at the research level, but also to the kind of educational aims that geographical education can help to achieve. For example is the comprehension of the concept of an ecosystem useful in achieving the environmental education aim?

Thirdly there is the problem of structuring a course in such a way that it ensures some progression of understanding so that geography can effectively help to stretch some young minds without putting others off. This is intimately linked to the problem of motivation for whereas the mind stretching process may be highly motivational for some students, it may have to be used with discretion with those whose intellectual development is at a different stage and who might easily be discouraged. Thus a course needs to be structured in a way that takes cognizance of what is known about the processes of mental maturation.

Fourthly there is the problem of devising the learning experiences, that is, the teaching units which are used by the teacher to enable the students to learn certain skills and ideas which dovetail into the overall geography course.

Fifthly there is the need to make this planning flexible enough so that it may be modified in the light of all kinds of feed back; feed back through tests, feed back from students' evaluation, feed back from colleagues, parents and so on.

My purpose will be not only to discuss various models of curriculum planning, but also to suggest a way of applying one such model to geographical education in the hope that it will be useful in practice. In so doing however, I am not advocating revolution in geography departments up and down Great Britain (or anywhere else for that matter). What is planned must be realistic and based on what is possible. It is much more likely that a gradualist approach will succeed in making curriculum changes, when an attempted revolution may cause chaos and little else.

# CHAPTER TWO

# Curriculum Models

## Introduction
In this chapter I want to look at what we mean by a curriculum model and examine in some detail two kinds of models: an objectives model and a process model. Each will be evaluated with a view to its utility in curriculum design and planning in geography. I also want to examine how far curriculum development teams explicitly make use of curriculum models in their work.

## The meaning of curriculum model
As indicated in Chapter 1, most traditional syllabuses in geography were largely lists of content. Thus implicitly those of us who were teaching to those syllabuses were assuming that our job was essentially to get the students to learn the content of the syllabus, though we accepted that we might also have other objectives in school, such as coaching a football team, or running a dramatic society or teaching morality incidentally. Although we were not necessarily conscious of it, we were behaving in a particular way in relation to our students and this behaviour could be represented by a model; that is a simplified representation of complex reality which enables us to understand this behaviour better. This model of our teaching behaviour could be shown to be at two levels: first at the general planning level, i.e. at the level of planning a whole course as shown in Figure 2.1.

Our starting point was to make certain overall assumptions about the aims of teaching geography. Put in another way we were averring that geography was worth teaching and learning because, for example, we felt that the information it gave was useful to future citizens, that it taught students to observe their environment more analytically, and that it developed certain skills such as map reading which

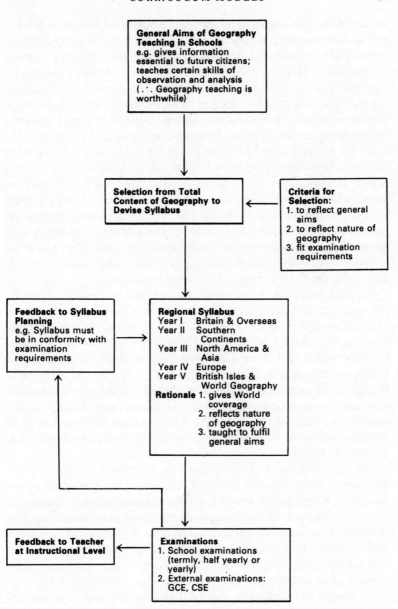

FIGURE 2.1 Curriculum process model at the general planning level.

would be directly useful in job or leisure pursuits. Armed with what was in fact a general justification for the teaching of geography we proceeded to construct a syllabus by selecting from the total content of geography. Because the current view (or paradigm) of geography was one which stressed areal differentiation (or the regional synthesis according to whether you looked at it through North American or European eyes), this syllabus tended to be a regional syllabus emphasizing the differences between one area and the next. One criterion for selecting the content tended to be that of assessing whether the content helped to fulfil the overall aims of the subject Still at the general level, one tended also to plan termly, halfyearly or yearly examinations or tests to see how far the students had learned what they were supposed to learn. True, the motives were many sided since these examinations also might help to motivate students as well as enabling rank orders to be established in a class. These and the syllabus were also devised with the external examinations in mind, especially the G.C.E. type, mode I examinations.

Now the feed back of tests and examinations to teachers about the performance of their students was at the instructional (i.e. at the level of planning particular teaching units) rather than at the general planning level. A model of the curriculum process at the instructional level is shown in Figure 2.2. Essentially it shows the pattern of decisions a teacher makes about his day to day 'lesson' planning in the light of (a) general criteria handed down from the general planning level and (b) feed back information from the way individual 'lessons' actually worked with his students. From the general planning level these could also feed back information about past external and internal examinations.

The main merit of such a model is that it attempts to make explicit the pattern of processes which go on in the formulation of a curriculum in the sense of actual teaching-learning activity. Figure 2.1 shows the pattern of the process at the more generalized level of planning the overall syllabus. It makes clear the kind of assumptions made and the criteria used in this planning. You will probably notice that the situation described by the diagram is not without possible conflict. For instance it may well be that external examination requirements are such as to make difficult the realization of some of the general aims of geographical education. Figure 2.2 shows how the curriculum process operates at the instructional planning level, that is it shows the decisions made by a teacher about how he is going to

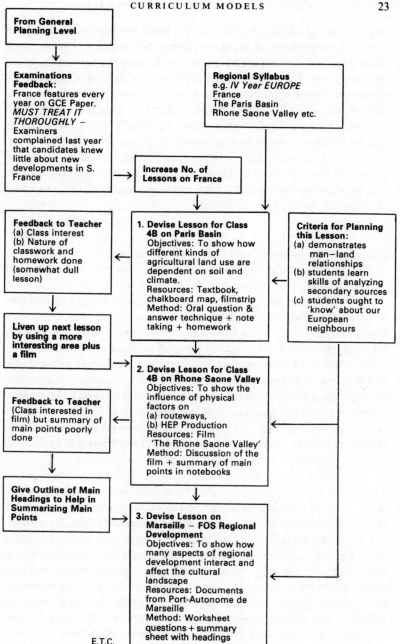

**From General Planning Level**

**Examinations Feedback:** France features every year on GCE Paper. *MUST TREAT IT THOROUGHLY* – Examiners complained last year that candidates knew little about new developments in S. France

**Regional Syllabus** e.g. *IV Year EUROPE* France The Paris Basin Rhone Saone Valley etc.

**Increase No. of Lessons on France**

**Feedback to Teacher** (a) Class interest (b) Nature of classwork and homework done (somewhat dull lesson)

**1. Devise Lesson for Class 4B on Paris Basin** Objectives: To show how different kinds of agricultural land use are dependent on soil and climate. Resources: Textbook, chalkboard map, filmstrip Method: Oral question & answer technique + note taking + homework

**Criteria for Planning this Lesson:** (a) demonstrates man–land relationships (b) students learn skills of analyzing secondary sources (c) students ought to 'know' about our European neighbours

**Liven up next lesson by using a more interesting area plus a film**

**Feedback to Teacher** (Class interested in film) but summary of main points poorly done

**2. Devise Lesson for Class 4B on Rhone Saone Valley** Objectives: To show the influence of physical factors on (a) routeways, (b) HEP Production Resources: Film 'The Rhone Saone Valley' Method: Discussion of the film + summary of main points in notebooks

**Give Outline of Main Headings to Help in Summarizing Main Points**

**3. Devise Lesson on Marseille – FOS Regional Development** Objectives: To show how many aspects of regional development interact and affect the cultural landscape Resources: Documents from Port-Autonome de Marseille Method: Worksheet questions + summary sheet with headings

E.T.C.

FIGURE 2.2 Curriculum process model at the instructional planning level.

organise his teaching on a day to day basis but again in the light of certain assumptions about the syllabus and certain criteria about objectives. The term 'objectives' is used here in the sense of short or medium term objectives in contra-distinction to long term aims. At the instructional planning level it is also evident that there is a good deal of immediate 'feed back' from students which allows the teacher to modify his plans for future 'lessons'. I put the word lesson in quotes because I am not implying any particular format or style of teaching, but simply a *'learning experience'* organised by the teacher. It is also clear that planning here involves being able to formulate objectives, use appropriate learning/teaching resources and organise a teaching strategy (or method, or approach).

### The objectives model of curriculum planning

The origins of this model are American and go back to the first quarter of the twentieth century when F. Bobbitt wrote *The Curriculum (1918)* and *How to Make a Curriculum (1924),* but really became well known when Ralph Tyler (1949) wrote his short but very lucid book *Basic Principles of Curriculum and Instruction.* I shall not go over this in detail since I have already done so in *Geography in Education* (1975). But the basic message was simple – education is a process which involves changing people's behaviour, therefore if you want to be successful in this activity, you must first be crystal clear about what kind of behaviour you wish to bring about. This is sometimes known as the linear model since it can be viewed as a sequence as shown on Figure 2.3 which is derived from Hilda Taba's development of Tyler's principles into practical curriculum planning.

The crucial aspect of this model is not the organisation of the content or learning experiences, but the formulation of the objectives. A good deal of work has been done in North America on the formulation of objectives starting with Bloom (1956) and Krathwohl (1964) in which a taxonomy of educational objectives in the cognitive and affective domains was developed, originally for the use of mental measurement. Further the development of programmed learning techniques also resulted in the development of behavioural objectives, that is objectives which carefully and precisely specify the kind of behaviour change required of the learner. In 1962 Mager wrote *Preparing Instructional Objectives* and later Popham (1969) and Gronlund (1970) also wrote on the same topic.

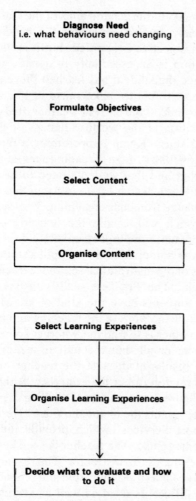

FIGURE 2.3 An objectives or linear model of curriculum planning (after Taba 1962).

The teacher might well welcome such precise objectives, since they give him closer guidance than do general aims or examination syllabuses. Let us look at what is implied by examining an example in the area of meteorology which has been provided by Kemp (1971) for 8 – 9th graders in the U.S.A. corresponding to 13 – 14 year-old students. Kemp's model is shown in Figure 2.4. The contents of each box are elaborated below.

Under 'Purpose is set out the general aims of the teaching unit, which are more specifically spelled out under the heading of 'Learning Objectives'. Each objective is justified, but it is interesting to note that this justification is an essentially pragmatic one. Apart from indicating that once the student has learned these particular objectives he will be better able to make sense of the weather maps in newspapers and to understand current weather, there is no attempt at an overall justification of the worthwhileness of the topic. Under 'student characteristics', Kemp is presuming a range of measured I.Qs, but none below 108, a range of reading ages, some knowledge of physics and weather and that students need to be challenged with individualized activities, which I take to mean that they would welcome or need a change from mass teaching. The 'subject content' is the knowledge which will enable the learning objectives to be achieved. In the present sample, objective No.4 (being able to identify local air masses) cannot be achieved until a student has mastered the characteristics of the main air masses and learned to identify each air mass 'in the field'. The 'Pre-Test' really consists of two tests, one to find out if the students have the kind of knowledge which will enable them to follow the work of the teaching unit (the pre-requisite questions) and the other is to find out whether some students do not already know some or all that the unit is meant to teach them. According to the results of the test the teacher may steer, certain students in one direction rather than another. Although it occupies only one box in Figure 2.4 (a) in fact 'Teaching/Learning Activities and Resources' represents the major activities in terms of time if one links it to 'Support Services' which provide the 'hardware' for teacher and students to use. The teacher is seen here as a presenter and manager rather than as an instructor. The resources involved are quite important in so far as a graphic artist and school media specialist (media-resources officer) is used as well as secretarial staffs. The 'evaluation' is a kind of post-test to see whether students have really achieved the learning objectives which have been set.

Clearly such a model is applicable at the instructional level and the learning objectives used may in fact be those devised by the teacher rather than by the curriculum specialist. These objectives tend towards, but are not quite, behavioural objectives as these are defined by purists. For example objective No.2 does not specify how accurately the source regions of air masses have to be labelled. If I place the Canadian Source region for continental polar air in the Lake St. John

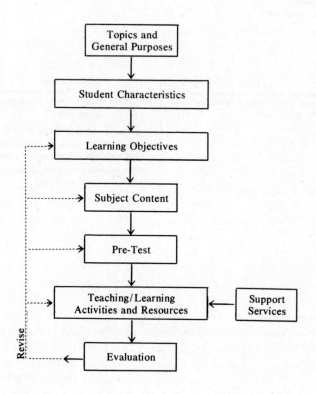

FIGURE 2.4(a).

FIGURE 2.4(b).

**Subject Area:** General Science
**Unit:** Weather
**Topic:** Air Masses

| PURPOSE | STUDENT GROUP |
|---|---|
| To know the characteristics and sources of air masses. | 60 advanced eighth and ninth graders |
| | IQ range: 108 to 137 |
| | Reading levels: 8th through 12th grades |
| | Students have some background in the unit and in physical science principles. |
| | Many students need to be challenged with individualized activities. |

FIGURE 2.4 — *continued.*

| LEARNING OBJECTIVES | SUBJECT CONTENT |
|---|---|
| 1. When given the name of an air mass to write its proper symbol with 100 percent accuracy.<br>*Justification:* In your reading, in our class work, and on newspaper weather maps, air masses are commonly referred to by letter symbols. To identify the various air masses, you should know and use these symbols.<br>2. On a map of the northern hemisphere to mark the source regions of at least three air masses and indicate their directions of movement in summer and winter.<br>*Justification:* The weather over the U.S. results from the movement of air masses across the country. Therefore, by knowing where each air mass originates and its method of movement, we can determine much about our weather.<br>3. When given temperature, humidity, wind direction, visibility, and cloud types, to name the air mass with 90 percent accuracy.<br>*Justification:* These are the characteristics that make each air mass unique. You will be able to identify an air mass by observing these weather conditions.<br>4. To observe local weather conditions and indicate the air mass affecting the area (with a class concensus of 80 percent).<br>*Justification:* You should apply your knowledge of air masses to practical situations. Often, one air mass moves into an area occupied by another one and mixing takes place. Therefore, we do not always find clear-cut indications of these characteristics. An 80 percent concensus is acceptable. | 1. Definition of an air mass: A widespread body of air with similar properties throughout.<br>2. Source regions:<br>(a) land—Alaska, Canada, Arctic.<br>(b) water—Gulf of Mexico, Caribbean Sea, Mid-Atlantic Ocean, North Pacific Ocean.<br>3. Designations of air masses:<br>(a) mP—maritime Polar.<br>(b) cP— continental Polar.<br>(c) mT—maritime Tropical.<br>4. General characteristics of air masses:<br>(a) tropical—warmer than the land below; high moisture content; poor visibility, stratus clouds; drizzle, dew; each mass moves generally north and east.<br>(b) polar—colder than the land below; low moisture content; good visibility; cumulus clouds; showers, thunderstorms; each mass moves generally south and east. |

FIGURE 2.4 — *continued.*

| PRE-TEST | ACTIVITIES AND RESOURCES |
|---|---|
| **Prerequisite Questions**<br>1. When cold air is heated from below, what happens? (One or more correct answers)<br> a. The air rises.<br> b. The air warms.<br> c. Strong vertical currents may be created in the air.<br> d. The air spreads out.<br> e. The air cools.<br>2. If air rises or is forced upwards, what happens? (one or more correct answers)<br> a. The air cools.<br> b. The ability of the air to hold invisible water vapour is reduced.<br> c. The air warms.<br> d. Any clouds in the air will disappear.<br><br>**Pre-test Questions**<br>3. What does each symbol mean?<br> mP    cP    mT<br>4. What area(s) may be the source region(s) for *tropical* air?<br> a. Gulf of Mexico<br> b. Southeast USA<br> c. Africa<br> d. Mid-Atlantic Ocean<br> e. Southwest USA<br>5. What are the characteristics of a polar air mass?<br> a. warmer than land, cumulus clouds<br> b. good visibility, showers<br> c. high moisture, poor visibility | The teacher will introduce the topic of air masses as a presentation to all students. The students will then follow the sequence of learning activities on their own. All students to complete the same activities. Each one will sign up for a discussion group when his activities are completed.<br><br>*Teacher Activities*<br>1. Present a five-minute animated film showing types of air masses, how each forms, source regions, and movement.<br>2. Use overhead transparency to review source regions. Indicate symbols used for air masses and show movement with arrows. (Handout sheet for student use.)<br>3. Participate with groups of 8 to 10 students to review activities and completed exercises, answer questions, and discuss local air mass conditions that day.<br><br>*Student Activities*<br>1. Follow presentation. Take notes on hand-out sheet that contains outline and details of content.<br>2. Study short filmstrip on air mass characteristics and weather elements. Follow instructions in accompanying programmed instruction booklet.<br>3. Each student will read two booklet reports on the effects of air masses on ground and flying conditions. Complete exercises with each booklet.<br>4. Sign up for discussion group.<br>5. Committees to make local observations on schedule for a two-week period. Report findings about air masses to class each week. |

FIGURE 2.4 — *continued.*

| SUPPORT SERVICES | EVALUATION |
|---|---|
| Budget: $25 for materials to prepare transparency, five copies of 14-frame filmstrip, printed materials, and five copies of recording. | 1. Beside each of the following, write the correct symbol: continental polar air mass maritime tropical air mass maritime polar air mass |
| Personnel: (1) teacher to present content to group and meet with small groups; (2) district graphic artist to prepare transparency and titles for filmstrip (4 hours); (3) district photographer to prepare and reproduce filmstrip (6 hours); (4) school media specialist to obtain recording from local airport tower and adapt it for student use; (5) school librarian to prepare and distribute materials; (6) teacher aide to duplicate recording and supervise independent study work; (7) secretary to type and duplicate printed materials. | 2. On the worksheet map, mark the source regions for all possible air masses. Use the name and symbol for each. Show the direction and extent of movement during summer with a solid line, and during winter with a broken line. 3. Listen to the tape recording marked 'Weather Reports.' You will hear three sample broadcasts to pilots in flight. Recording A: Is this a continental polar or maritime tropical air mass? Recording B: What flying conditions would you expect in this air mass? Recording C: What is the name and symbol for this air mass? |
| Facilities and schedules: large-group presentation room for 20-minute module; small-group meeting room for six 30-minute meetings; five independent-study carrels for two days (estimate one hour of study time per student). | 4. Observe today's weather. What kind of air mass is affecting our local area? Justify your answer with at least four facts. |
| Equipment and materials: 16mm projector; short animated film from district film library; overhead projector with one transparency; 5 filmstrip viewers with copies if 14-frame filmstrip; 5 cassette tape recorders with copies of three-minute recording; 1 transparency handout sheet for each student; 5 programmed instruction booklets; 12 reports on air masses and exercises. | |

Source: Kemp, J. E. (1971), *Instructional Design,* Fearon.

area in Quebec, am I right? Nevertheless, the objectives are likely to be specific enough for most teachers and most students. The question which may be raised is 'How does this particular Unit fit into the geography curriculum and the total school curriculum?' This is a question which I hope to answer in Chapter 3.

Meanwhile you might enquire about the utility of this objectives model of curriculum planning at the instructional level. At first, a teacher might argue that such a model is perhaps over elaborate and too formalized for an activity which often goes on with much informality, and seldom in the fairly rigid manner which the diagram in Figure 2.4(a) seems to indicate. This is equivalent to saying that the day to day reality of teaching geography may not much resemble what is shown in the diagram. Or you might object that what happens does not necessarily happen in the way indicated on Figure 2.4(a). For example you may find yourself considering your students before deciding on the 'general purpose', since you estimate that certain objectives would not be achievable with these students. Or again you may feel that you know your students well enough to dispense with the pre-test sequence. Or again you may argue that you do not have available the resources and support services postulated by the teaching unit on air masses. All these I would class not as fundamental objections to the model, but modifications to it brought about by the particular circumstances of the teacher and his students. In other words you could argue that in the planning of instruction, a teacher might behave in a way similar to that indicated by the model and that if his behaviour was wildly different, then he might well improve his planning if he used the diagram as a 'model'.

Objections to the 'objectives' model are really objections to its blanket use in all situations. It is argued that it fits quite well the training situation where the student is learning a particular skill, e.g. how to measure slopes with an abney level and two ranging poles, or how to test soil for pH value. It is also argued that the objectives model is appropriate when instruction involves the learning of well established scientific or other principles, for example, learning the principle that the interaction between two towns will be the greater, the greater is each town's population and the smaller their distance apart. In both these cases it will help the teacher to define as closely as possible what kind of behaviour he wants his students to acquire. This is fine except that there is clearly a sense in which teaching reaches its ultimate objectives when student behaviour departs from what was predicted. The student who goes beyond the prescribed objective, who sees the limitations of a principle or theory and who solves a problem in an original unprescribed way, is the student whose education has been a great success. Thus in so far as teachers ultimately hope that some students will become original and creative thinkers, it would be wrong to limit their instruction to pre-specified objectives. In practice it is probably difficult to stop someone from thinking in a creative manner, though it is true that he may be discouraged. Thus the teacher who uses an objective model needs to be aware that some of his students will go beyond the objectives he has set, indeed they may well outpace the teacher's thinking. It may hurt the teacher's self-esteem to recognise this, but it is important not to stifle creative thinking. In spite of all these warnings, an objectives model for curriculum planning in geography is, in most cases, appropriate.

In some aspects of geographical education it would be inappropriate to use, an objectives model. For example, recent studies in 'perception geography' involve the student in finding out what others perceive as most significant in a landscape. It would consequently be wrong to pre-specify what they should find out! Similarly, where games and simulations are used, as in the case of the 'North Sea Oil game', it is difficult to prescribe behavioural outcomes. It has also been argued by Sockett (1976) that, in any case, the idea that behavioural objectives can be specified without ambiguity is probably an illusion, since one can never be sure that a response to a question given by a student means precisely to him what it means to the teacher. There is therefore always an element of uncertainty about the outcome of a learning experience – what is planned does not necessarily materialize no matter how tightly defined are the objectives. Another possible problem is that because the evaluation process is closely linked to the objectives in the total structure of the model, only those objectives which can be measured will be aimed at. This is a serious objection to the blanket use of the objectives model. Lastly, those purists who insist on strictly behavioural objectives, may find that this involves defining a very large number of objectives for a small teaching unit. So much energy may be spent on delimiting precise objectives that little is left to devise the learning experiences. A more limited but useful attempt to specify objectives in geography in the Junior Secondary School has been undertaken by the South Australian Education Dept. (1978).

## A process model of curriculum planning

In order to overcome the objections to the objectives model particularly in the area of the disciplines of knowledge, Stenhouse (1975) has proposed what he calls a process model. As I understand it, such a model concentrates not on objectives but on procedures, and on the process of learning. In other words it is concerned not with the precise matter learned by the student but with the kinds of procedures for acquiring knowledge that the students may learn. Let us take a geographical example. Suppose that one is concerned with the topic of 'population geography', which can be described as the spatial aspects of population, namely population distribution, population growth in relation to regional resources, population migrations, and so on. An objectives model might start off by specifying in some detail the kinds of ideas that the students ought to learn; birth rate, death rates, fertility rates, net-reproduction rates, density of population, push-pull causations of migrations, exponential growth models, etc. A process model of curriculum planning would shift its interest to what teachers and students do in order to reveal some of the procedures necessary to tackle the problems inherent in the content chosen. In the case of population geography the kinds of problems which arise are those of over-population, of racial tension in areas where two or more ethnic groups co-exist in spatial continguity, of concentrations of under-privileged groups in certain urban areas, etc. Teachers and students must then decide how they can obtain information to illuminate the problems, how reliable this is, how they can analyse this information, what conclusions they can draw from it, what proposals could be made to alleviate the problem. The ultimate result of the teachers' and students' activities is not *a body of knowledge,* but an *ability* to find information, criticize it, analyse it, assess its value, and formulate a solution to the problems posed. Incidentally concepts and principles will be learned, for example, the concepts of birth rate, death rate, density of population, as well as the reasons causing one rate to fall, another to remain constant and so on. In detail, this model of the curriculum process places value on students posing their own questions, on students learning elementary research methodology and how to look up first hand information and assess its worth as evidence, on students learning to discuss by listening to others as well as putting their own arguments forward, on students learning that knowledge is not finite but open-ended, and on students learning to look upon the teacher not as an authority but as a guide or resource. Since the teacher is no longer looked upon as the authority on knowledge, he becomes a 'senior – learner' able to offer advice on information sources but also aware of the nature of his own subject, its position in the total structure of knowledge, its philosophical position and methodology. His main function is to develop understanding in depth rather than the attainment of limited knowledge objectives. The teacher's ability to be an acceptable critic and to interact profitably with his students is seen as vital in this model. Consequently, the teacher must be committed also to the idea of seeing his own teaching as problematic, he must be committed to acquiring the skills for studying his own teaching, and lastly sufficiently committed to putting those skills into practice and to allow others, students and colleagues, to observe and criticize him.

Stenhouse (1975) rightly poses the question 'Will a process model work in practice?' He does not directly answer his question. What I would like to do is to describe such a model in diagrammatic terms (Figure 2.5) so that it may be compared with the objectives model. It is of course my own interpretation of what I believe Stenhouse means.

At first glance there is not an enormous difference between the two models if one thinks in terms of planning. Both are at the instructional planning level, both set out to devise learning experiences, both make use of subject content and of resources, and both set out to evaluate the result. The main differences lie in the nature of the objectives and in the nature of the evaluation. In the first place the 'learning procedures to be developed' in the first box of the process model (Figure 2.5) are more in the nature of general aims than the precise behavioural objectives set out in the objectives model. This is how Stenhouse and other like-minded curriculum theorists would have it. The question then arises as to whether these are sufficient guidance for the teacher. For example what kind of research skills can one expect seventeen-year-old students to develop? How precise should be their formulation of a problem?

In the second place, whereas the objectives model as designed by Kemp uses post-tests in the evaluation procedure, in the process model the evaluation is much wider and includes self criticism by the teacher, the opinions of other teachers and students as well. This means that a good deal of the evaluation must be subjective in one form or another.

My own view is that the model offered by Kemp is not a model

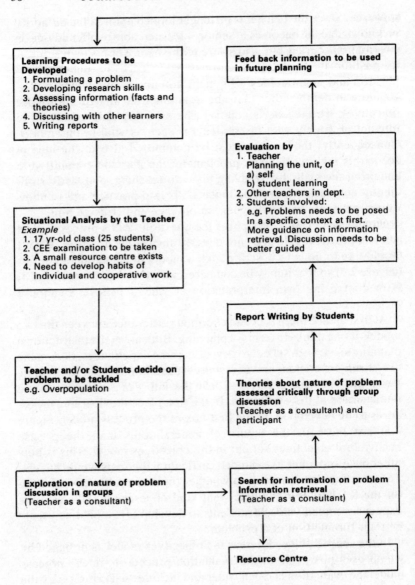

FIGURE 2.5. An interpretation of Stenhouse's curriculum process model.

applicable in all its detail, at least not in the present context of secondary education. It involves a degree of specific detailed planning of objectives, pre-tests and post-tests which would tax a teacher's energy without correspondingly benefiting the students. This is not to say that an objectives model is not useful for planning certain aspects of the geography curriculum, but I would doubt the value of developing behavioural objectives in the extreme form in which they are often stated, and the utility of evaluating every teaching unit in the detail postulated by the model. On the other hand the process model seems to be singularly devoid of precision as to content. Its aims as stated in Figure 2.5 are really suitable for what I call the general planning level rather than the instructional level. In other words one can bear in mind when planning instruction that these general procedural aims need to be implemented, but they give little guidance as to which content to include, except, of course, that it must be content capable of exploitation along procedural lines. But for what other reason should the teacher have chosen to use the problem of over-population rather than that of atmospheric pollution or transport harmonization is not clear. This is also true of the objectives model which gives no overall criteria for choosing content.

## Curriculum models and curriculum development

Since my contention is that we all have a curriculum model of some sort to work by, even if this is held at the sub-conscious rather than at the conscious level, it is likely that curriculum development teams will have used explicit rather than implicit models since they are likely to be aware of the issues involved in curriculum design. Further since the teams were and are concerned with the geography curriculum, one can expect that content guidelines would have been considered in some depth. Indeed this is what we find. The American High School Geography Project (1961–70) was concerned with content relating to urban structure and urban processes, the location of industry, agriculture land use patterns, cultural and political areal differentiation and spatial interaction, ecological equilibrium and regional analysis. Similarly, the Schools Council's 'Geography for the young school leaver project' (GYSL) spelled out its content interest in some detail in the three main themes for which it provided teachers' guidelines and materials, namely 'Man, land and leisure', 'Cities and peoples' and 'People place and work'. The project team also gave the criteria on which these themes had been chosen. The other two British projects, 'Geography 14–18' and 'History, Geography and Social Science 8–13' were less inclined to lay down clearly the content areas with which they would deal. It is true that the 'Geography 14–18 project' negotiated a special examination at O level with the Cambridge Local Examinations Syndicate and to that extent had to specify some content, but on the whole the project team was disinclined, except by way of exemplars, to detail the kind of content which was deemed appropriate. The contrast between the two groups of project is interesting because it is a manifestation of two models of curriculum development. The American High School Geography Project and the Geography for the Young School Leaver project both subscribed to an objectives type of curriculum planning model at the instructional level, though not with behavioural objectives. This is clear if one reads any of the materials provided for teachers by the projects. On the other hand, 'Geography 14–18' and 'History, Geography and Social Science 8–13' were both projects which emphasized that a curriculum could not be planned without taking into account the important variables of the teacher who was going to implement it and the school environment in which it was to be located. Thus both projects were virtually affirming that the curriculum cannot be changed without changing the teacher. This is also Stenhouse's (1975) position, who affirms his faith in the 'teacher as a researcher'. Thus, the argument goes, if only the teacher can be turned into a curriculum developer, then curriculum development based on explicit curriculum theory will take place, which as on *a priori* argument is no doubt infallible. But the hard reality is that teachers do not, indeed cannot, become curriculum developers without content.

It might be objected that I have somewhat shifted my grounds, and that I am now dealing with curriculum development rather than curriculum planning. The two are inextricably mixed at the present time. It is, of course, possible to envisage curriculum planning for a static curriculum, a kind of efficient management of a 'saber tooth curriculum' (Benjamin 1939). But all I have written on the objectives and process models of curriculum planning so far indicate clearly that these models refer to a dynamic rather than a static curriculum.

To return, then to the apparent opposition between the objectives and process models of curriculum planning, I would argue that the differences between them are ones of emphasis rather than of substance, and that the emphasis put on objectives may best suit one situation and the emphasis on procedures may best suit another. Both seem to have relevance in geography since they have both been used by different curriculum development teams. My natural inclination would be to combine them into an eclectic objectives and process model of curriculum planning at the instructional level. But a model for the general planning level is also required. I shall deal with both these models in the next chapter.

# CHAPTER THREE

# Suggested Models for Planning the Geography Curriculum

## Introduction

In this chapter I would like to argue for simple models of curriculum planning which may help teachers to design their geography curriculum. By designing I do not mean a 'grand design' in which everything is thought out anew and revolutionized, because as indicated earlier, things do not work that way in schools and society. Rather are these instruments which he can use to modify his curriculum from year to year or day to day according to the situations which arise. First, I will consider the 'general planning level' and all that this implies in relation to general aims; paradigms of geography and examination. Secondly, I will look at the 'instructional planning level' and the associated problems of content, resources, and teaching strategies. It should be clear that what follows are suggestions which could be tried, not prescriptions. For a model of the administrative processes involved in curriculum planning for the whole school the teacher is referred to Bates' (1973) article in *Decision making in British Education*.

## Preliminary considerations

Since education and schooling involve value positions, it is essential that my own values are evident. I accept the distinction between schooling and education in the sense that Peters (1966) makes it. That is all that goes on in school is not education if you define education as 'initiation into worthwhile activities'. Stenhouse (1975) analyses the formal activities that go on in school as belonging to four categories; *training, instruction, initiation* and *induction*. There is little confusion about the first two terms which cover training for particular skills, and instruction aimed at transmitting particular facts, principles or theories. Initiation is concerned with what sociologists would call the 'expressive' order of the school, its values, rituals and norms; 'induction' Stenhouse uses to cover the process of developing an understanding of thought processes, of the methods of particular disciplines, so that the learner begins to acquire what Peters described as cognitive perspective. In general, a truly educated person would be one who had not only received training and instruction but had acquired such cognitive perspective. It is important to bear in mind that in ordinary usage education and schooling are often used interchangeably and that for many people the really valuable part of schooling (to them) is the training and instruction which they received. It is interesting in this context to note the situation in Western Europe in the nineteen-seventies where the 'mind opening' process of education was deemed inadequate, if it did not at the same time provide some training and instruction which would enable school and university students to find employment. To some extent the reaction against 'progressive' education can be understood in similar terms. Of course, the distinction between instruction and education need not be a hard and fast one, since some instruction is likely to cause students to ask questions, seek relationships, and develop new ideas. Much depends on the spirit in which instruction is given, whether as a system of closed or open knowledge. The teacher, it seems to me, has commitments to all aspects of schooling and not just to developing 'cognitive perspective'. Certainly, in teaching geography he will be training in skills, instructing in principles, as well as opening minds to the implications of certain spatial aspects of society, for example spatial social segregation. I would go as far as stating that though developing 'cognitive perspective' is a necessary part of the process of education it is not in itself sufficient.

The second value statement, implicit in the writing of this book, is that I believe in the necessity for some overall planning. There has been a tendency among some curriculum developers to argue that since each school, each student, each teacher is unique, the organisation and planning of the curriculum must be left to the individual who knows the situation at first hand. In one sense this is true, since only the teacher on the spot can make curriculum plans into reality. But most teachers are not super men or super women, they welcome some assistance in what is a time-consuming and arduous task. Thus, what I am proposing is not to take the task out of their hands, but rather to give them tools which may save time and labour. The choice of content is still theirs and so is the classroom application. There is no doubt that the quality of the educational experience of students is dependent on the quality of the teachers who interact with them. So why not let the teachers concentrate on this interaction process and give them as much help as possible in the planning of their courses? This is, of course, assuming that curriculum planning is a rational activity and that teachers wish to undertake it in full knowledge of the options open to them.

### The general planning level

At the general planning level few curriculum models for geography have yet been developed, at least not explicitly, though many syllabuses have been proposed. Syllabuses have the disadvantage of being static lists of content, thus inevitably unsuitable for a dynamic curriculum situation. At best they can serve as a source of content for incorporation into the curriculum process. My general planning model then is an instrument for choosing content and specific objectives for the instructional level, based on criteria which are at a high level of generality. It is represented diagrammatically on Figure 3.1.

It is, as suggested earlier, a combination of an objectives and process model in that it begins by assuming certain overall educational aims and then looks at the process of translating these into a school course, which itself is influenced by such factors as examinations and what is known about the psychological development of students and the sociology of education.

Let us take each box in turn. I will not dwell on the aims of schooling and education since these have already been discussed to a limited extent and there exists a monumental literature on these. The word aims has been placed in inverted commas because in relation to Peters' definition, education is a process which cannot have an aim since it is an activity which is worthwhile in itself (Peters 1965). However, since schooling is instrumental to ends beyond itself, it is perhaps permissible to use the term 'aims'. Within my first box, I therefore include personal development as well as training and instruction. In order to fulfil these general aims, it is necessary to select one or more appropriate paradigm(s) of geography (Box 2). A paradigm can be looked upon as a model of geographical research and

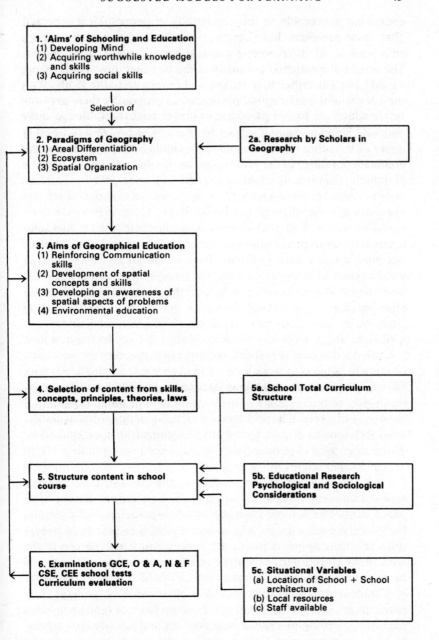

FIGURE 3.1. Model for curriculum planning in geography at the general level.

endeavour acceptable to the community of geographical scholars. Three such paradigms have been put in the second box since there are adherents to all three among professional (research) geographers. The areal differentiation paradigm is the one that most geographers would have subscribed to in Britain and France up to the 1950s. With the advent of the conceptual revolution in geography there are now fewer adherents to this paradigm in higher education, though there may still be many among school teachers. The problem is whether either of the other two command sufficient loyalty to be seen as the dominant paradigm in the profession, or whether one has to accept a pluralistic situation. It might be argued that since man-land and/or environmental problems are still a major concern of geographers that the ecosystem paradigm gives a better fit than the spatial organisation paradigm which, though it has numerous adherents in the U.S.A., has a narrower outlook and tends at the secondary school level to leave out pure earth-science problems from its purview. For schools, I would select at the present time the ecosystem paradigm since it provides for a smoother transition from the erstwhile areal differentiation paradigm. You will note however, that there is a feed back loop from the examinations box, since clearly if your department subscribes to an examination which requires regional description then you will need to select areal differentiation as a paradigm or select two or more paradigms to work with, or change your examination board. Courses for students not taking examinations will be unaffected by this aspect of the feedback. This is a situation in which conflict will have to be resolved. The problem is that it may be difficult to make the areal differentiation paradigm fulfil the general aims of education. Those interested in pursuing this theme should read Biddle's (1976) article on 'Paradigms in Geography'.

From the paradigm chosen will come the kinds of aims of geographical education in particular (Box 3). You cannot choose aims which cannot be derived from the paradigm selected. For example, the spatial organisation paradigm cannot yield aims such as 'developing a scientific appreciation of the natural landscape'. Some of the aims I have chosen derive from the ecosystem paradigm others would be common to other paradigms as well. I would argue that in geography students learn, as they would in other subjects, general communication skills such as reading for comprehension (and sometimes pleasure!), writing to expose both feelings and knowledge (expressive, even poetic and transactional writing), and numerical and mathematical skills. More specifically geography is concerned with developing children's and adolescents' spatial concepts and skills particularly in relation to mental operations concerning phenomena at the local, regional, national and world scales. What I mean by this is developing students' ability to conceptualize different kinds of space so that they can move about in the space with appropriate mental maps, rather than with inadequate or poor-fit mental images. Important skills related to this ability are first, those of keen observation in the fields of what will become significant features of the mental map, secondly those of map making and map reading, particularly the ability to use a map in the field and to translate relevant information on a map into a mental map, again to enable the student to move about and orient himself successfully in the environment. Another purely geographical aim is that of developing an awareness of the spatial aspects of human problems. This in effect means developing in students the ability to observe spatial regularities and to seek explanations for these. For example, the regularities of field patterns in the North American Prairies or St. Lawrence Valley, the spatial regularities in urban areas, regularities in rural settlement, in rural land use and so on. The problem aspect lies in the planning of future land use. Lastly, I would argue that geography must involve itself in environmental education, though it will clearly not be the only subject to do so. Environmental education involves adopting a value position with respect to various aspects of the environment and being conscious of, and understanding, the ecological or other relationships involved. In an urban society we are probably aware of the environmental issues within towns, but these need to be analysed and a commitment entered into. Such an aim is directly related to the ecosystem paradigm of geography.

Having accepted a series of general aims it is necessary to select the kind of content which may make possible the achievement of those aims (Box 4). You will note that I have stated the content will be in terms of skills, concepts, principles, theories and laws; this is deliberate because in spite of the still popular notion that 'geography is about countries', it is not possible, in my view, to justify fulfilling the aims of geographical education through a descriptive factual content. Although it is not appropriate here to go into the detail of content, this being done in Chapter 4, an example of each type is given. An example of skill is that of matching aerial photographs and medium scale map information which would satisfy the aim of developing spatial skills; an example of a concept would be that of central business district (CBD) which would aid the development of an awareness of urban spatial regularities and of town planning problems; an example of a principle would be that of the friction of distance again affecting the understanding of spatial regularities; an example of a theory or law would be Huff's formulation of the probability of the shopping behaviour of individual shoppers according to their home location and that of supermarkets in the area; again this would be a theory helping to explain spatial regularities or spatial behaviour. Studies of environmental perception may help to fulfil the environmental education aims of geography, since it is vital to know how students view an environment before attempting to work on their attitudes to it.

The drawing up of a list of possible content is a useful step forward, if only because a good deal of unnecessary content will have been eliminated in the process, that is content which could not achieve the aims postulated. For example there is a vast literature on regional geography only a fraction of which will be directly useful to the teacher planning his work. Moreover, the same general objectives can be achieved with a selection from a range of content. The content list needs structuring into a viable course or courses (Box 5). This is where psychological and sociological considerations come in. Perhaps certain sociological considerations should not be considered. It might be argued that the same process of education must be applied to all irrespective of social background, otherwise we might get into a situation in which one kind of geography was taught to working class children who are expected to underachieve and another type to middle class children who are expected to overachieve. Many would argue that this is a description of present day reality and that something ought to be done about the situation. How does it arise? The process is insidious and takes the form of a two way interaction. Teachers find that students have difficulty in coping with the work and gradually adjust their demands until the students appear to cope. But the students finding that teachers expect less of them adjust their performance downwards. The process then becomes a vicious circle of low teacher expectations and low student performance, first revealed experimentally by Rosenthal and Jacobson (1968), and which can be exacerbated by streaming which labels children as able or less able in a year group.

Inevitably the existence of different courses for different examinations or for non-examination students makes for a variety of curricula in geography for different groups. Not only are there variations between different G.C.E. boards, but there are at O level alternative syllabuses within a single board. Further, C.S.E. examination boards may offer Mode I, Mode II and Mode III examinations each with a different syllabus; many Mode II and Mode III syllabuses may exist within a single board. The result is differentiation of curricula and a tendency for a hierarchy of courses to be established with non-examination courses at the bottom of the hierarchy and G.C.E. O level at the top. This may also lead to an unequal allocation of teachers and resources as between the various levels. Attempts to cope with this problem have led to the development of mixed ability teaching and/or individualized learning in the lower school. But this belongs to the instructional level. My own inclination would be to attempt to structure a common course involving choosing overlapping CSE and GCE O level courses, with, however, plenty of latitude at the instructional level for the teacher to adjust to the situation he finds. For as Bruner has pointed out, it is not so much that certain ideas are inaccessible to some students, rather is it that the same ideas need to be learned in a manner meaningful to those particular students. I am not suggesting that the process is easy, nor that teachers will not be faced in certain situations with total incomprehension, not to say, hostility. But in such a situation, no amount of tinkering with the structure of a course will do any good. What is required is a changed attitude on the part of the students or of the teachers and this may not be easy to achieve. Much depends on the rapport the teacher is able to build up with his class as well as on the total atmosphere of the school. In many inner urban areas, the teacher may have a long uphill task of making student attitudes favourable to the education process as a whole, let alone to geography in particular.

Psychological considerations are no less complex but they are less intractable, for it is a little clearer in what ways they affect the course structure. First and foremost there is a need to develop favourable attitudes at the beginning of the course among the younger students. This involves not only organising activities, such as field work, which they are likely to enjoy, but also making sure that the content has concrete meaning for them. I have dealt elsewhere with the significance of Piaget's work to geographical education (Graves 1977), in this context it is sufficient to indicate that the stages of mental development of students must influence the course structure. In a

British context, I would argue that it means the following:

1. Until the ages of 14—15 years most students are still for most purposes at the stage of concrete operations. This means that the course must to some extent follow an inductive method and be based on concrete examples. Thus the concept of hinterland should be dealt with through a case study of, for example, Hamburg or New Orleans, rather than through an *a priori* definition of hinterland.

2. Theoretical propositions must be introduced carefully, and largely in the last two or three years of the five-year secondary course, since these require essentially hypothetico-deductive thinking. Thus Huff's formulation of shopping behaviour mentioned earlier, probably belongs to the last year of the course or the Sixth Form.

3. Problem situations need to be posed from the beginning, but the factors involved must be few in number to begin with. Even by the age of 16, quite able students find a multi-variable situation difficult to handle, so that dealing with four or five factors will probably tax their thinking sufficiently. This is very important because so many problem situations in geography are very complex and involve a multitude of variables. It is often necessary to artificially limit the size of a problem to make it usable with secondary school students.

Another way in which psychological considerations affect the nature of the course is to make it conform to Bruner's notion of the spiral curriculum idea — that is to develop an idea gradually and in a different form from the first year of the course to the last, gradually examining the complexities of the idea and its theoretical aspects. One need only think of the way the concept of the field of influence of a town may be studied by twelve-year olds (where do the shoppers come from?) compared with how it may be considered with eighteen-year olds (how do you delimit a field of influence of a small town?) to understand the idea.

Although geography is not redolent with many instances, there are concepts and ideas which logically precede others, where later ideas are not comprehensible unless the earlier ideas have been tackled. An obvious example of this is Reilly's formula for calculating the breaking point between the fields of influence of two towns; such a technique can have no meaning until the ideas behind 'fields of influence' have been assimilated.

The way in which the school geography course is structured is clearly affected by the manner which the school's total curriculum has been organized. At present two broad structures exist in the secondary school:

1. Geography is a separate subject throughout the school course.
2. Geography is part of a combined course (humanities, integrated studies, environmental studies or any other title) for the first two or three years, and then becomes an independent subject for the rest of the school course.

If the second structure applies, then the geography curriculum planner will need to take account of the other subjects contributing to the common course and plan cooperatively. He will need to ensure that basic ideas and skills in geography are included. This is all the more important as less time will probably be available for geographical content. The course structure will also be influenced by such situational variables as the location of the school and its access to various resources.

The problem is now posed as to whether any particular framework needs to be used to structure the content. Traditionally, content has been arranged within a regional or systematic, or thematic or concentric framework and protagonists have argued about the merits of each. I am inclined to believe that most overstate their case and that the particular framework used is less important than the quality of the teacher-student interaction. However, I am willing to go as far as to express a preference for a thematic framework rather than no framework at all. I rationalize this preference by arguing that at the research level geography is largely thematic in the sense that professional geographers elect to study for example urban problems, or medical geography or rural settlement patterns and so on. Further, those themes often correspond to problem situations in society on the spatial aspects of which geography may throw some light, and as such, students may see some purpose in the framework used. Indeed one American geographer (Clyde Kohn, in press) has argued that the geography curriculum should be based entirely on the solving of 'real' problems. The difficulty lies in reconciling the needs of the theme with the need for progressive growth in cognitive understanding. The last box in Figure 3.1 is merely there to recognize the mutual interaction between content and the tests and examinations which are used by teachers. In so far as students take internal school tests or Mode 3 examinations (i.e. set and marked by teachers but externally moderated) then the problem is not a difficult one since the tests and examinations attempt to evaluate what the geography curriculum has provided. One needs to be aware, however, that the kind of examination or test used has an inevitable effect on the curriculum, for example objective tests will lead to teachers stressing the kind of knowledge tested by those tests, therefore it is important to use a wide variety of evaluation techniques; course work assessment, essay topics, project assessment as well as objective tests. Truly external examinations have the same effect except that because the teacher is not in control of the examination process, he can only adjust his course to meet examination requirements. Changing the examination can be an extremely slow process. We have already noted the potential for conflict which exists. Within the last box (6), the term 'curriculum evaluation' indicates that teachers may evaluate the course by other means than those of examinating or testing their students. The views of the students themselves may be sought either informally or through a questionnaire. Similarly, the views of teachers who teach the course will need to be taken into account. It may also be useful to seek the opinions of such 'outsiders' as research or professional geographers, educationalists and last, but not least, parents. What can or cannot be done in curriculum evaluation lies in the realm of practical politics (For curriculum evaluation see Hamilton *et al* 1977).

### The instructional planning level

Here we are concerned with the month by month, week by week, and even day by day planning process. Planning at this level needs to be based on the content suggested by the general planning level and yet be flexible enough to adjust to what may be important but passing events. By this I mean that an event in the school, in the locality or even at national or world level might result in the teacher abandoning the planned curriculum for a while either because the event is of intrinsic importance to the students e.g. a major landslip in the locality, a flood, the building of a new road, and/or because of the motivational value of the event e.g. the Israel operation in retrieving the hostages held by terrorists at Entebbe airport Uganda in July 1976.

A model for curriculum planning in geography at the instructional level is suggested in Figure 3.2.

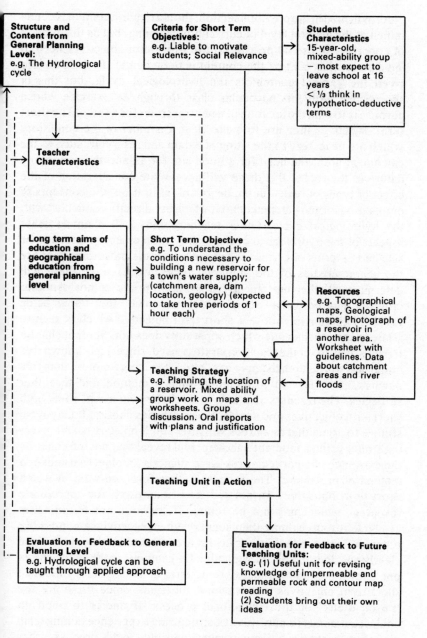

FIGURE 3.2. Model for curriculum planning at the instructional level.

As indicated in the previous section, the curriculum content is determined at the general level of curriculum planning, but as this is a list of concepts, skills and principles, the short term objectives need to indicate in what context the content is to be taught. In the example given the general content is the hydrological cycle, but this is approached with this particular class through an exercise whose purpose is to plan the location of a new reservoir for a town. The short term objectives then are to make clear a number of the conditions which are necessary to the siting of a dam and reservoir, such as the catchment area, the need for a good site for a dam, the underlying nature of the rocks. But these will necessitate consideration of the effect of types of rocks on the degree of infiltration, the concepts of drainage basin and catchment area which are directly connected with the hydrological cycle. Other teaching units will examine other aspects of the hydrological cycle – short term objectives need to be selected in terms of certain criteria of which the most important are the characteristics of the students to be taught, since these will determine whether the objectives are appropriate or not. Another criterion may be that of social relevance, since other things being equal it is better to choose a short term objective which is seen to relate to society than one which apparently does not. Student characteristics also affect the teaching strategy used, since if it is known that one group will seldom listen to expository teaching for more than five minutes, it is as well to abandon such a method and try other strategies. The teachers available to teach the course will affect both short term objectives and the teaching strategies chosen. It may seem strange to argue that resources will affect both objectives and teaching strategy, but a moment's thought will reveal that not infrequently the existence of a particular resource suggests an objective and/or a method of procedure. The process is therefore two-way, in which short term objectives formulated lead to a search for appropriate resources which may not be found. If they are not found other available resources may then suggest other objectives and possibly other strategies. Teaching strategies are affected by resources since clearly one does not use moving film, for example, in the same way as one uses topographical maps. Long term aims must also influence short term objectives and teaching strategies, since these are the 'raison d'être' of the educational process. If one is to open up adolescent minds to new ways of structuring experience (a long term aim) then short term objectives must contribute to this process rather than concentrate on factual learning. Similarly, the teaching strategy must incorporate means of making the student develop and practise those intellectual skills which the long term aims postulate. In the case illustrated in Figure 3.2, the students are expected to study evidence about the relief, geology, and river flows in the area concerned, and to come to some decision about where a dam and reservoir may be located. This involves discussion in groups and making an oral report, so that besides the specific short term geographical objectives to be achieved, one expects also the achievement of certain of the general educational aims which appear in Figure 3.1, such as acquiring worthwile intellectual and social skills. In terms of the general geographical long-term aims, this teaching unit is concerned to develop an 'awareness of the spatial aspects of a problem'. It also gives scope for students being creative, in the sense that they can suggest ideas – the problem to be solved does not admit of only one solution. This is brought out in the evaluation of the unit.

A difficulty which always arises when using an applied problem of this sort is that issues will be raised which go far beyond the short term objectives of this unit and which may not be directly related to the content area from which the unit is derived. For example, as a result of considering the possible location of a reservoir, the students may raise issues concerned with land use conflicts. These strictly belong to another aspect of content. These issues may have been dealt with earlier, in which case their recapitulation in such an instance serves as reinforcement. If they have not already been covered, then it would seem appropriate to air them not in the present context, but to await the opportunity of discussing these in full later under the appropriate content heading. In the ultimate analysis only the teacher can decide what to do in a given situation. With a generally poorly motivated class of students, any issue which seems to attract their interest is probably worth pursuing.

You will have noticed that I use the term 'short term objectives' rather than behavioural objectives. This is because the kind of objectives I propose are not behavioural in the strict sense of the term. They do not prescribe that students shall be able to behave in a strictly defined way at the end of a teaching unit. Nevertheless, they describe with some degree of specificity the kind of understanding which it is hoped the students will acquire.

Lastly, although this is not shown in Figure 3.2, the way the curriculum process actually operates will depend on the kind of interaction which goes on within a geography department and on the total climate of the school. If the climate is an authoritarian, closed one, there may be little room for manœuvre in the curriculum planning process.

## An example

The example is taken from the content area of coastal geomorphology and is concerned with coastal erosion involving cliff undermining, rotational slip, the effect of lithology and rainfall infiltration on the stability of coastal cliff forms. It is expected to take one-and-a-half to two hours of teaching. It is proposed to plan a teaching unit for a group of first-year-sixth formers (seventeen-year olds) who are offering geography at 'A' level in the G.C.E. These students are reasonably able to think in a hypothetico-deductive manner, but only about a quarter intend to pursue geography any further. Most intend to study economics or one of the arts subjects in higher education. Motivating them is still of some importance. The short term objective is to get them to understand that cliff erosion is not just a matter of the sea undermining the cliff foot, but is aided by lithological and climatic considerations. A criterion for selecting these objectives is that coastal erosion management is a live issue in many areas of Great Britain and the world, but particularly in densely populated areas.

Apart from standard textbooks on geomorphology and coastal processes, another resource is a useful article, ('Barton does not rule the waves' by M. J. Clark, P. J. Richetts and R. J. Small – *Geographical Magazine,* July 1976) which is a case study of a particular cliff collapse involving damage to protective sea defences, gardens, private houses and hotels. The article documents the history of coastal erosion and the attempts to prevent it as well as the events of the cliff collapse of 1974/75. It contains a map, a diagram and several photographs. The teaching strategy will be to give each student a copy or photocopy of the article and to ask them to describe:

    (a) the sequence of events in the cliff collapse,

    (b) the kinds of processes which were at work,

    (c) what special factors helped to aggravate the situation,

    (d) why coastal protection measures failed to do their job in spite of the enormous investment?

A second aspect of the teaching strategy will be to ask students to discuss the authors' concept of environmental management and in what ways economic and technical issues interact.

A third aspect of the strategy would be to simulate a discussion between representatives of the owners of property threatened with demolition by cliff collapse, councillors for the local district council, a consultant geomorphologist, a consultant engineer and a consultant economist. This would also be a useful way in which the teacher could evaluate whether the students have fully grasped the issues involved.

Long term aims would be those of environmental education as well as those of developing the ability of students to obtain information from sources and assess this information.

## Summary

The main purpose of this chapter has been to outline two models of curriculum planning in geography: one at the general planning level and one at the instructional planning level, indicating also the links between the two levels. The models are meant to be instruments which enable teachers to select content, objectives, resources and teaching strategies appropriate to the kind of circumstances in which they find themselves. Although examples of content and courses are given in the appendices to Chapters 4 and 5 respectively, it is *not* suggested that these can be taken over lock, stock and barrel by teachers irrespective of their school circumstances, or indeed of teacher's own personal strengths and predilections.

# CHAPTER FOUR

# Selecting the Content of School Geography

## Introduction

The selection of the kind of content with which the teacher can attempt to reach both his short term and long term objectives is probably one of the most difficult of the curriculum planning task. It is difficult largely because of the 'embarrassment of riches' which exists. The vast content of geography means that the selection process can sometimes be painful, since there may be no strong reason why one body of content should be chosen rather than another. For example, we can demonstrate the kind of conditions which lead to the development of twilight zones in towns by focusing on the issue in one town or by looking at urban processes in general. We can do this by looking at London, New York, Singapore, or Sydney. What we can no longer do is insist that our students should know about the precise nature of the 'twilight zone' problem in all the main world cities. There is thus a problem of selecting the concepts, principles and skills which are worth teaching (the content proper) and the kinds of examples which may be used to illustrate them (the context). There is also the further problem of deciding which ideas and skills are appropriate to a particular group of students' stage of mental development. Should the ideas be limited to those where concrete examples can be readily found to demonstrate them, or should the teachers be stretching the students by considering the general implications of an abstraction like 'spatial diffusion'. Over and above these theoretical considerations, there are a number of practical constraints which operate, such as the length of the course, the amount of time available, the kind of resources at the teacher's disposal and the staff's interests and capacities, not to mention the current attitude of pupils. Let us first look at the general structure of courses.

## Course structure

Although there are theoretically a large number of possible combinations of courses on a secondary school timetable, a pattern is beginning to emerge in England and Wales which is fairly widespread. If we consider the 'secondary school years' to cover the age range 11 to 19, then this divides into three stages. The first stage consists of the first three years of secondary school (11 to 14+) where in some areas pupils are placed in a separate 'middle school'. The second stage consists of the next two years (14+ to 16+) where school students are following courses in preparation for the G.C.E. 'O' Level and/or the C.S.E. examinations, though some may not be sitting for any examination. The third stage (16+ to 19+) is that where students staying on beyond the compulsory years of education are following a two-year (sometimes three-year) course to sit for the 'A' level (or 'N' and 'F'?) examination. Some students stay for only one year in the sixth form to sit 'O' level examinations previously not taken or failed and some are taking the C.E.E. (Certificate of Extended Education) or the alternative 'O' level examination. Those who stay for a third year may be either those who wish to compete for a university scholarship or those who having completed 'O' level subjects in the first year of the sixth form, then continue with a two-year 'A' level course. The sixth form years (16+ to 19+) may of course be spent in an 11+ to 19 secondary school, in a sixth form college or in a college of further education.

During the first three years of secondary schooling, geography is usually taught in some form or other, but the main division is between those schools which teach it as an independent subject and those which teach it within a group of combined subjects usually known under such titles as 'integrated studies', 'environmental studies', 'humanities', 'modern studies', 'world studies' and so on. It is not my purpose here to appraise the educational value of such combined studies, but to indicate that planning the geography curriculum in such a course comes under three additional constraints. One is the relatively smaller time allocation likely to be given to the geographical element in the curriculum. Another is the need to negotiate with other members of the team teaching such a curriculum, the appropriate content to fit in with the non-geographical aspects of the total course.

Yet another is the fact that the geographical element in such a course may be taught by non-geographers.

In general, the first three years of the secondary school course are free from the limits imposed by external examination syllabuses and question papers, and are therefore the years in which a good deal of experimentation with different types of content can be undertaken.

In the second stage, geography is usually taught as a separate subject, though about 50 per cent of students opt to take other subjects. In the third stage, geography is a specialist subject in a three (or five) subject curriculum.

This division into three stages of the secondary school curriculum has certain advantages from the point of view of content selection. The first stage (11+ to 14+) corresponds largely with a period when pupils are still mainly in the stage of 'concrete operations', to use Piaget's terminology, although some (a minority) will have crossed the threshold into 'formal propositional thought' in a number of areas of knowledge. This means that the content will need to deal with relatively simple 'concepts by observation', (e.g. a river terrace), simple functional relationships or statements where the concrete examples are evident (the larger the town, the greater the number of its retail functions), and simple skills not involving complex mathematical understanding (e.g. bar graphs). It also implies that the kind of examples used must be those which may be found mainly in the locality of the school or in the national area and less frequently in Europe and more distant lands, though admittedly the use of film and television helps to give students reasonably accurate second experiences of distant lands. The need is to build upon personal or vicarious experience until such a time as pupils have a strong basis of conceptual thinking which enables them to make comparisons with phenomena in areas they do not know at first hand.

The second stage (14+ to 16+) corresponds to the period when hypothetico-deductive modes of thought begin to develop for many students, though many will still find a theoretical proposition difficult to understand. It is during this stage that some 'concepts by definition' can be successfully introduced (e.g. the location quotient), where relationships of a slightly more complex nature may be taught (e.g. the decision of a farmer to specialize in dairy farming is a result of his perception of the interplay of such factors as soil, climate, market and government policy), and where somewhat more complicated skills may be introduced (e.g. proportional divided circles). The curriculum may be more-or-less tightly guided by examination requirements depending on the kind of examination that students sit for at the 16-year-old level.

The third stage (16+ to 18+ or 19+) is one when mental development enables the student to handle more abstract situations and where the self motivation of intellectual pursuits may be much stronger. Students' analytical powers develop and make them aware of the limitations of certain propositions and theories. In other words, their critical faculties are sharper and they can be initiated into the idea of knowledge as problematical rather than certain. They can therefore handle much more difficult concepts (e.g. the threshold population for a service function) and more elaborate principles (like Reilly's principle for working out the breaking point between two towns' fields of influence) as well as understand the purpose and operation of such a skill as the computation of the Spearman-Rank correlation coefficient. They also become aware of the relationships between various parts of geography and between geography and other subjects. Thus the significance of a geographical point of view or of spatial awareness begins to mean something to them.


**The classification of content**
Given this sub-division of the secondary school course into three stages, is it possible to arrange the content of geography in an appropriate manner?

First it must be borne in mind that any course must be based on certain aims and that a variety of content may achieve the same aims. For example, general aims such as those of developing map reading skills may be achieved using a wide variety of maps. But even if one becomes more specific and develops such objectives as making the student capable of working out the accessibility of a town in a road network, there is still a wide range of maps which can be used for this purpose at different scales of different countries and so on. Secondly, the total content of a subject may be organised in a variety of ways according to the system of classification used. Thus, the traditional way in which Human Geography was divided was to use such headings as Agricultural Geography, Industrial Geography, Urban Geography, Rural Settlement; or again Regional Geography (often ostensibly the only form of geography in schools), Economic Geography, Social Geography, Political Geography. Physical Geography was

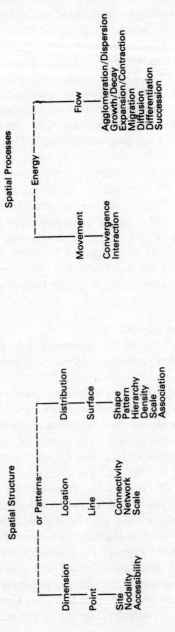

FIGURE 4.1.

usually divided into Geomorphology, Climatology and Biogeography. Today, although these classifications are still used, one often sees the content of geography categorised as belonging to Earth Science, Man Land Relations, the study of Areal Distribution; of Areal Differentiation, Spatial Interaction and of Regional Analysis. As an alternative, human geography is often described as being concerned with spatial patterns and spatial processes and teachers have sometimes attempted to subdivide these into a series of concepts, as did Cromarty (1975) in Figure 4.1, which is based on Haggett's *Geography, a Modern Synthesis* (1972/75).

Other schemes of subdividing the ideas of Geography exist (Ghaye 1977), though each scheme overlaps with another. One emanating from a conference of Geography teachers in Australia (Education Department Victoria 1975) suggests some sort of hierarchical arrangement of the content of geography as shown on Figure 4.2.

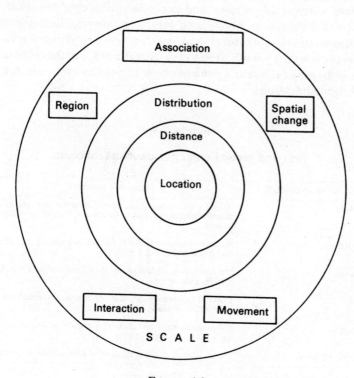

FIGURE 4.2

The logic behind the diagram on Figure 4.2 lies in the fact that location must be understood before the distance between locations can be measured; that the idea of space measurement involving distance must be acquired before the distribution of phenomena on space can be apprehended; that all three ideas must be understood before spatial interaction, areal association, areal differentiation (how regions differ), movement through an area or spatial change through time can be meaningful. On the other hand, each organizing concept in the outer circle is to a large extent independent of the others in this outer circle. Thus while one needs to know about location, distance and distribution to understand 'spatial interaction', one does not necessarily need to understand 'spatial change through time'. Scale is a concept which applies at all levels. A similar kind of idea exists in the scheme outlined by Walker (1976) and represented in Figure 4.3. It is a modification of Broek's (1965) view of geography's main organizing concepts.

Here a series of primary and secondary concepts are used to structure a course in which such topics as farming, industry and communications, settlement and environmental problems give a focus to each year's work. It has very clear themes, but the disadvantage of limiting each year's work to one or two topics such as industry and communications.

FIGURE 4.3.

**First and second order geographical concepts**

| Primary concepts | Secondary concepts |
|---|---|
| Location | Position and distribution; areal specializations; regions; association/segregation of functions; least cost/optimum location. |
| Interaction | Man and the environment; factors influencing locations and links; trade; aid. |
| Distance | Efficiency of route; actual distance, time and cost distance; effects on locations. |
| Scale | Scale of representation; scale of operations/problems; economies of scale; hierarchies. |
| Change | Diffusion of ideas and methods; growth and decline; sequent occupance; inertia. |
| Representation | Maps, graphs, photographs, diagrams, statistics, models. |

Source: *Teaching Geography*, Vol. 1 No. 4, Tables 2 and 3.

Figure 4.3 (Continued)

## A conceptual syllabus in human geography

CONCEPTS

EXAMPLES ON VARIOUS SCALES: Local———world.

| Themes | Location | Interaction | Distance | Scale | Change | Representation |
|---|---|---|---|---|---|---|
| Local Area and Land Use in Britain. | Location of points [co-ordinates, grid refs, lat. and longitude]; location of areas —types of towns, zones in towns, land use zones; spheres of influence. | Factors influencing zoning in towns and countryside, need for conservation. | Straight line, road and time distance; route planning [shopping and road journeys] | Measurement of scale, use of scale on maps. Hierarchy of shopping centres. | Changing patterns of land use and building styles. | Maps, graphs, photographs, diagrams. |
| Farming. | Agricultural land-use patterns. | Factors influencing land use—relief, soils, climate, distance, scale of operations, government actions and human attitudes and knowledge; trade. | Effect on land use, both on a farm and in terms of distance to a market. | Scale of operations, eg size and organization of farms. | Changing patterns of agricultural land use. | Maps/topology, graphs, photographs, diagrams, models. |
| Industry and Communications. | Location of industry. | Factors affecting location of industry—raw materials, power, labour, markets, capital, individual and government actions and chance. | Effect on least-cost locations. | Economies of scale influencing location. | Changing patterns of industrial location; industrial inertia. | Maps/topology, graphs, diagrams, models. |

(Continued Over)

## Continued — A conceptual syllabus in human geography

### CONCEPTS

| Themes | Location | Interaction | Distance | Scale | Change | Representation |
|---|---|---|---|---|---|---|
| | Networks. | Factors influencing types of networks—distance, type of goods, etc; trade. | Accessibility; route efficiency; time and cost distance. | Size of flows and routeways. | Changing networks. | |
| Settlement. | Types of settlements; siting, urban zoning, spheres of influence. | Factors influencing siting of settlements, and functional zoning—resource availability, chance, association and segregation, distance, government and individual actions etc. | Effect on spacing of settlements, range of goods and services, etc., efficiency of route. | Hierarchy of settlements. | Changing functions of settlements; changing patterns of urban land use. | Maps, graphs, diagrams, photographs, models. |
| Environmental Problems. | Location of developed and developing countries; distribution of pop., location of productive and unproductive land, areas subject to natural disasters, areas of natural beauty, etc. | Man as a part of the ecosystem—need for conservation; factors influencing the stage of development; aid. | Effect on diffusion of ideas, and level of knowledge. | Scale of world problems—of population and food supply, pollution, etc. | Changing technology; changing attitudes. | Maps/topology, graphs, diagrams, photographs, models. |

EXAMPLES ON VARIOUS SCALES: Local———world.

It would seem to me advantageous to allow the first three years of the secondary school course to be as open as possible. This means that topics chosen need not conform solely with the traditional concerns of geography, though the examples chosen would tend to be those which pupils could relate to their own experiences. This would imply some constraints as to the kind of phenomena studied and their location, but not as to the topic. By this I mean that any topics or themes that seemed appropriate may be studied, but that the level at which each is studied must depend on the teacher's judgment of what is possible and desirable with the group of pupils he has to teach. Thus when a pupil is studying urban land use, he can be observing that there is more commercial activity in town centres than on town peripheries, without going into bid-rent curves or Ricardian theory of rent. My own view is that there is no need to have an overall theme for each year of study. No such overall theme or themes exists in the teaching of any other subject as far as I am aware, and the nature of geography does not require them. Pupils are no more impressed by 'year themes' than by any other schemes; they are much more likely to judge a course by their daily or weekly experiences in the classroom, in the laboratory or in the field. This is not to say that groups of 'lessons' should not be linked through a theme, problem or topic approach, but rather to imply that long periods of study on farming or communication or industry have no special merits particularly in the 11–14+ age range. It is up to the teacher to decide on the theme, topic or problem which will best serve the purpose of teaching the principles, concepts and skills he has as his main objectives.

Another more simple way of clarifying content is given by Burton-wood (1976). He suggests using six organizing concepts, namely:

1. PATTERNS IN GEOGRAPHY
   The key concepts of land value, distance, gradient and decision making will be studied in the context of rural land use patterns, urban land use patterns and settlement patterns. The emphasis in this part of the course will be on the U.K. but other regions will be included for comparison, e.g. the South American City.

2. BEST LOCATION
   The concept of best location will be applied to studies of power stations, the steel industry (U.K. and U.S.A.), the cotton industry in Lancashire, airport location, residential zones in London and village sites in New Guinea.

3.  NETWORKS
    The concepts of accessibility, centrality, and connectivity will
    be applied to transport networks in the Lake District, Sardinia,
    Snowdonia, Scotland and the U.K. motorway system. The
    skills required will include topological transformation, matrix
    construction, the calculation of the Beta, Gamma and Detour
    indices and the drawing of time distance maps.

4.  SPATIAL VARIATIONS IN ECONOMIC DEVELOPMENT
    The concept of cumulative causation to be applied to:
    1. the regional problem in the U.K.
    2. the regional problem in Italy
    3. the under-developed world
    Emphasis will be put on problems of industrialisation, infra-
    structure, trade investment and aid.

5.  SPATIAL SYSTEM
    Emphasis will be on man's ability to apply technology to the
    solution of environmental problems. Sample studies will be
    made to demonstrate the man-land implications of:
    1. shifting agriculture in Africa
    2. extensive commercial agriculture in North America
    3. intensive commercial agriculture in Europe
    4. intensive subsistence agriculture in Asia

6.  SPATIAL INTERACTION
    Interaction is to be studied as movement between locations in
    response to spatial variations. The environment as perceived is
    to be stressed. Interaction is to be studied in relation to:
    1. journey to work
    2. migration
    3. world trade
    4. world communications.

In this example, the main organizing concepts are convenient headings under which various concepts and principles may be listed. They
do not in themselves summarise the main ideas of geography. For
example the heading 'Patterns in geography' is applicable to networks, since networks form patterns. Further, patterns are the
results of processes, thus it is difficult to study patterns of rural land
use without at the same time looking at the processes which brought
these patterns into being, but these are contained under the 'spatial

systems' heading. It may well be that in teaching such content, there is no attempt to teach it in the order indicated and that a good deal of mixing of categories is involved. It is useful, however, to see how a secondary school teacher views the content to teach to a group of students aiming at a C.S.E. examination in geography.

## Deriving content from the ecosystem paradigm

Since I have expressed a predilection for the ecosystem paradigm on the grounds that it provides a way of linking natural systems with man-made systems and therefore provides continuity with an older form of geography, I will attempt to derive content in secondary school geography from this paradigm. The ecosystem also has the advantage of making possible the achievement of the general aims of geographical education which I earlier postulated (Fig. 3.1), namely that geography seeks to develop:

1. the communications skills of literacy, numeracy and graphicacy in conjunction with other school subjects.
2. spatial concepts and skills, that is the ability to orientate oneself in the field as well as the ability to carry out mental spatial operations with maps and other representations of three dimensional space.
3. an awareness of the spatial aspects of problems, that is getting the habit of looking for the spatial implications of problems, for example the spatial implications of boundary changes in local government reform.
4. an awareness of environment and environmental problems, so that students are not only conscious of what their present environment is like, but capable of seeing the impact of a development proposal on the environment.

Diagrammatically the ecosystem paradigm may be represented as on Figure 4.4. That the content of geography is seen to be divided into two broad categories: natural systems and man-made systems, with links existing between each. The word system is used to indicate that each aspect is seen as dynamic rather than static and made up of interacting elements. Thus one uses the term biotic system rather than flora and fauna (or natural vegetation and its associated animal life). Each system within the two main categories clearly divides into sub-systems not shown on the diagram. For example, the geomorphic system contains within it sub-systems concerned with peri-glacial processes, costal erosion processes and so on.

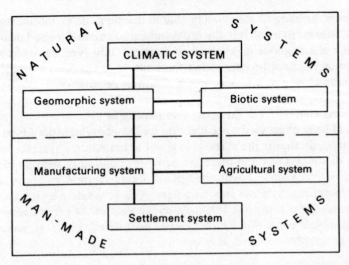

FIGURE 4.4

The problem is to structure some of the content into a course which seeks to achieve the aims postulated, within the constraints imposed by a school or college. Many of the variables to be considered are peculiar to a school or college, consequently these must be left to the teachers concerned. At the general level at which I am considering content, I shall attempt only to indicate the kind of content which might be used emphasizing the progression from the simple to the more complex, through the three stages of the school/college system. The word content is used here to indicate the concepts principles and skills which might be taught and not the context of teaching these. For example, the idea of shifting cultivation is content, but if it is taught by means of a case study in Africa, then this refers to the context. There is no implication that *all* the content must be used to achieve the general aims. Indeed in so far as most students will not ultimately become geographers, the content is only there to initiate them with the kind of spatial and environmental problems that geographers are engaged in attempting to solve. The concept of the 'compleat geographer' at 16+, 18+ or any other age is not a realistic one. The content is arranged in tabular form at the end of this chapter in such a way that new ideas are introduced each year. This does not mean that old ideas are not revised or their understanding deepened. Neither does it imply that an idea such as that of industrial linkages, allocated to the third year of the course, must never be mentioned before. The table is there as a guide to the kinds of concepts and principles which might appropriately be introduced and discussed in the years indicated. Map skills in the sense of the skills of reading and interpreting large scale and medium scale maps have not been given a specific column since I see these as integrated in the course during the acquisition of the substantive concepts. Maps are, after all, simply stores of information of a spatial kind, they are not part of substantive geography.

## Summary

In this chapter an attempt has been made to grapple with the problem of the content of geography which may be used to achieve the general aims of the secondary school geography course. This has been done by assuming (1) that the secondary school course would be divided into three parts (a) an 11+ to 14+ three-year section, when geography may be taught on its own or within combined studies, (b) a 14+ to 16+ section leading to a C.S.E. or 'O' level (or combined 16+ examination) (e) a 16+ to 18+ 'sixth form' course leading to 'A' level (or 'N' and 'F' level) after two years or to a C.E.E. or the 'A' ('O') level examination after one year.

(2) that the ecosystem paradigm as illustrated in Figure 4.4 provides a satisfactory basis for structuring the content of geography as it exists today. I am aware it is not the only possible framework and that a number of alternatives exist, for example, that given by the Oxford and Cambridge Examinations Board Commissioned Group for the N.F. study which suggests a break-down into (1) spatial awareness, (2) awareness of the natural environment (3) awareness of the man-made environment and (4) regional awareness. My own preference for the ecosystem subdivisions is that they correspond to some of the traditional concerns of geographers and of society.

It is important to bear in mind that the content listed in the tables is not meant to be the outline of a course, but merely a content resource from which the teacher might choose appropriate elements. In planning a curriculum in detail the teacher will need to give attention to objectives and teaching strategies as indicated in Figure 3.1 and Figure 3.2. No attempt has been made to specify the areal context in which the ideas, skills and principles may be taught or to suggest the way in which, in any given year, the various elements of the course might be dovetailed into one another. To some extent this must be left to the teacher, though some ideas on this will be given in the last chapter.

# Appendix to Chapter Four
## Possible Content of Geography Courses
## Using the Ecosystem Framework

### CLIMATIC SYSTEM

*STAGE I GEOGRAPHY OR COMBINED STUDIES*
*Year 11 – 12*
1. Weather observations with and without instruments and simple recording, e.g. state of sky, wind direction, wind speed temperatures, rainfall.
2. Seasonal changes in weather and its elements.
3. Variations in weather spatially – e.g. as between E and W and N and S in U.K.

*Year 12 – 13*
1. Variations in air temperature with altitude.
2. Simple convection cell – land and sea breezes.
3. Air humidity and evaporation.
4. Relief and convectional rainfall.
5. Graphical representation of mean monthly temperatures and rainfall.
6. Calculating mean monthly rainfall and mean monthly temperature.

*Year 13 – 14*
1. Representation of weather data on maps.
2. Insolation in relation to latitude and length of day and night.
3. Concepts of isotherm, isohyet and isobar.
4. Fog and temperature inversion.
5. Regularities in weather patterns e.g. desert areas, equatorial climate areas, mid-latitude continental areas.

## STAGE II GEOGRAPHY
### Year 14—15
1. Weather meso-scale systems, e.g. anticyclones, depressions, their representation on weather maps;
2. Concept of an air mass and its characteristics; the measurement of air pressure and ascending and descending air.
3. Convergence and divergence between air masses at ground level and above ground level;
4. Thunderstorms and tropical storms, e.g. cyclones, hurricanes and typhoons.

### Year 15—16
1. Concept of climate and climatic classification, criteria used;
2. Elementary treatment of the atmosphere as a closed system with energy transfer from equatorial to polar regions, Hadley cell, polar cell and the meridional circulation, zonal circulation, their relationships to meso-systems.

# GEOMORPHIC SYSTEMS

## ROCKS, NATURAL FEATURES, GEOMORPHIC PROCESSES

### STAGE I GEOGRAPHY OR COMBINED STUDIES
#### Year 11—12
*Observation* and *description* of (1) local physical features — e.g. valleys, spurs, plateaux, scarps etc; use of incomplete field sketch to name features; identification of features on a contour map; (2) rivers, lakes, seas, estuaries, confluences, source (if available at first hand) (3) river erosion, transport, deposition; (4) rocks, e.g. clay, sand, sandstone, limestone, chalk; (5) rock weathering; (6) sea action on beaches; (7) wind action on sand and other rocks.

#### Year 12—13
(1) *Classification* of natural scenery into plain, hill and mountain scenery according to elevation, morphology and scale; (2) slope measurement, e.g. scarp and back slopes for contrast; (3) Nature of a scree (talus) slope and of mechanical weathering; (4) Mass movement; (5) simple hydrological cycle (evaporation, transport of water

vapour, clouds, rain, run off); (6) sedimentation and the nature of sedimentary rocks; (7) river sediments alluvial plains and river terraces; (8) wind and sand dunes; (9) sea action and cliffs.

*Year 13 – 14*
(1) Permeability and porosity characteristics of rocks, aquifers; (2) rocks as sources of raw materials and energy; (3) rock structures faults, anticlines, synclines; (4) volcanoes, igneous rocks and earth movements, rift valleys, introduction to plate tectonics; (5) nature of chemical weathering; (5) high mountain scenery (glaciers, aretes, corries, U-shaped valleys, horns) and simple glacial processes (ice movement, abrasion, plucking); (6) more complex aspects of the hydrological cycle (infiltration, storage, springs, evapotranspiration); (7) river features, e.g. meanders, braided channels, nature of banks, waterfalls; (8) sea waves and longshore drift.

## STAGE II GEOGRAPHY
*Year 14 – 15*
(1) Granite bosses and metamorphic rocks (slates, schists, marble etc), minerals associated with metamorphic rocks (copper, lead, zinc, silver, kaolin); (2) river régimes and factors affecting this, nature of movement of water in a river; velocity of water in relation to channel form and gradient; (3) relationship between velocity, volume and load of a river; (4) River drainage patterns – dendritic, trellised – relationship to land surface and rocks; (5) scarpland topography; (6) Landscape of glaciated lowlands and glacial deposition, e.g. outwash sands and gravel, ground moraine, (7) coastal scenery in relation to (a) rock structure and relative land and sea movement, e.g. concordant and discordant coast, fjords and rias.

*Year 15 – 16*
(1) Classification of macro-relief features into: (a) Lowland sedimentary (b) Alpine type (c) block mountains (d) volcanic features; (2) recognition and classification of rocks into (a) sedimentary (b) igneous and metamorphic; (3) the hydrological cycle in relation to the drainage basin, the idea of the hydrological cycle as a system; (4) the idea of landscape evolution, the concept of dynamic equilibrium at meso-scales; (5) Macro-scale changes; earth and sea movements – classification of past earth movements – Caledonian, Hercynian and Alpine; (6) Concepts of glacial and peri-glacial landscapes.

# BIOTIC SYSTEM

## STAGE I GEOGRAPHY OR COMBINED STUDIES
### Year 11–12

1. Identification of trees, bushes growing in the locality, e.g. oak, birch, elm, chestnut, plane, gorse, broom, heather, fern, bracken.
2. Identification of such soils as clay, sand and loam soils.
3. Identification of common crops, e.g. wheat, barley, oats, root crops, cultivated grasses.

### Year 12–13

1. Mapping vegetation on a large scale map, i.e. concept of a vegetation map.
2. Recognition of vegetation associations, e.g. birch, broom, conifer and gorse on heathland, or moorland associations, or oak woodland.
3. Soil profiles: humus layer, A and B horizons.

### Year 13–14

1. Recognition of broad vegetation patterns on a macro-scale, e.g. from photographs: broadleaf forests, coniferous forests, savannah grassland, temperate grassland, Mediterranean, semi-desert and tundra vegetation types.

## STAGE II GEOGRAPHY
### Year 14–15

1. Relationship between soil vegetation and climate in, e.g. coniferous forest, temperate grassland and Mediterranean areas.
2. Introduction to the ecosystem idea, e.g. in the equatorial rainforest.
3. Equilibrium and change in the ecosystem.

### Year 15–16

1. Plant successions and the concept of a climax vegetation.
2. Man's influence on plant communities, e.g. fire, overgrazing.
3. Man's influence on soils, e.g. soil erosion, soil conservation.
4. Effect of drainage and irrigation on vegetation.

# AGRICULTURAL SYSTEM

## STAGE I GEOGRAPHY OR COMBINED STUDIES
### Year 11−12
1. Case studies of farms and holdings, e.g. dairy farm, arable farm, beef cattle farm, mixed farm, market garden and classification of farms.
2. Simple land use mapping on a scale of 1/10,000 in rural area.
3. Simple input/output model of a farm system.

### Year 12−13
1. Physical constraints on farming: weather, slope and altitude, aspect, soil, drainage; how constraints differ in different cultures.
2. Concept of subsistence farming constrasted with commercial farming.
3. Agricultural systems in developing countries: shifting cultivation, nomadic pastoral system, small scale settled food production − e.g. in Nigeria; identification of tropical food crops, cassava, yams, rice, plantains.

### Year 13−14
1. Classification of commercial farming systems:
   (a) tropical plantation system e.g. rubber plantation
   (b) intensive temperate mixed farming system
   (c) extensive grain farming system
   (d) extensive animal rearing system.
2. Overcoming physical constraints in farming:
   (a) irrigation, e.g. for swamp rice, for fruit growing (b) glass and plastic house horticulture (c) terracing.

## STAGE II GEOGRAPHY
### Year 14−15
1. Constructing divided circles to show land use.
2. Classification problems in agricultural land use (several crops per year, lay grass), L.U. maps.
3. Planning agricultural land use and decision making by farmers; how the similar physical areas may be used differently.
4. Problem of scattered holdings − the concept of farm consolidation.
5. Agricultural land use intensity around an urban centre (Von Thunen).

*Year 15—16*
1. Farmers' perception of the environment and of natural hazards.
2. Cultural attitudes to farming; land use conflicts.
3. Intensive commercial farming and environmental pollution.
4. Government agricultural policy and the farming system, e.g. the C.A.P.

## MANUFACTURING SYSTEM

*STAGE I GEOGRAPHY OR COMBINED STUDIES*
*Year 11—12*
1. Simple input/output model of a local factory.
2. Elementary analysis of site and its advantages and disadvantages.
3. Location of site using 6 figure grid references.

*Year 12—13*
1. Influence of raw materials on industrial location — e.g. iron and steel industry.
2. Influence of transport on industrial location, e.g. canal, railway, roadside and airport locations.
3. Power resources for industry: coal, gas, oil, nuclear H.E.P. Comparative uses and advantages, finite v. renewable resources.

*Year 13—14*
1. Factors influencing industrial concentrations, linkages and external economies of scale. Inertia or momentum.
2. An industrial region as an open system.
3. Problems of locating (a) thermal power stations (b) H.E.P. stations (c) nuclear power stations.

*STAGE II GEOGRAPHY*
*Year 14—15*
1. Elementary industrial location theory: the respective influences of market, raw materials, labour supply.
2. Decision making in industrial location:—a simulation.
3. A special case of industrial concentration: large ports.

*Year 15—16*
1. Distribution of industry in a national area; the location quotient.
2. Industrial location policy by governments.

3. Land use conflicts in industrial location.
4. Industrial pollution problems: smoke, effluent, radio-active hazards and their spatial and environmental implications.

## SETTLEMENT SYSTEM 1  POPULATION

### STAGE I GEOGRAPHY OR COMBINED STUDIES
*Year 11−12*
1. Population bar graphs of local towns.
2. Population by age groups (pyramids).

*Year 12−13*
1. Reading distribution of population maps.
2. Physical factors influencing distribution of population.

*Year 13−14*
1. Birth rates, death rates, natural increase, graphs of population growth.
2. Density of population and factors affecting this.
3. Population classification into language and ethnic group.

### STAGE II GEOGRAPHY
*Year 14−15*
1. Problems of population statistics — reliability of collection; size of enumeration area.
2. Making a dot distribution map, and a choropleth map.
3. Concept of urban and rural population.
4. Population migration and some of its effects.

*Year 15−16*
1. Population growth rates and resources — differences in the developed and developing world.
2. Elementary consideration of the demographic transition model.
3. Population growth and economic development.
4. Population migration.

## SETTLEMENT SYSTEM 2   SETTLEMENT

### STAGE I GEOGRAPHY OR COMBINED STUDIES
*Year 11−12*
1. Elementary land use mapping in urban area around the school, classification of residential and commercial properties.

2. Differences between rural and urban settlement.
3. Locating towns by latitude and longitude.

*Year 12–13*
1. Village sites and functions: historico-spatial considerations.
2. Simple classification of town centre functions, shoppers' goods, convenience goods.
3. Evidence of town growth by age of building.
4. Original site of towns.
5. Concept of sequent-occupance.

*Year 13–14*
1. Size of town and its functions.
2. Concept of the field of influence of a town.
3. The spacing of towns, regularities.
4. The environmental quality of towns: how to gauge this.

## STAGE II GEOGRAPHY
*Year 14–15*
1. Urban structure: various models.
2. Urban development processes.
3. Urban hierarchy and the rank size rule.
4. The concept of new towns.
5. Ports and their hinterland; a special case of the field of influence.

*Year 15–16*
1. Urban growth in the developed and undeveloped world compared.
2. Urban planning and urban renewal.
3. Land use conflicts in urban areas.
4. Urban dwellers' perception of towns.
5. Administrative divisions and city-region concept.

## SETTLEMENT SYSTEM 3  NETWORKS

## STAGE I GEOGRAPHY OR COMBINED STUDIES
*Year 11–12*
1. Local bus routes, nodes and edges.
2. Classification of forms of transport, advantages and disadvantages.
3. Measuring movement or flows.

*Year 12 – 13*
1. Planning a journey (a) within a town (b) between two towns.
2. Location of such nodes as railway and bus stations.
3. Journey to work: mapping flows; the commuter problem.

*Year 13 – 14*
1. Catchment area of local bus service;
2. Road networks and accessibility;
3. National air networks – longitude and time;
4. Rail network – adaptation to changed conditions.


## STAGE II GEOGRAPHY
*Year 14 – 15*
1. Integrated transport network: Competition and complementarity.
2. The integration of a network; the $\beta$ index and connectivity.
3. Airport location problems.
4. World air routes and the International Date Line.
5. Spatial interaction: traffic between towns, simple gravity model.

*Year 15 – 16*
1. Road traffic within towns: patterns, problems, possible solutions.
2. Concept of a trade network, international trade links of a nation.
3. Political manifestation of trade network: E.E.C., G.A.T.T.


## GEOMORPHIC SYSTEM

## STAGE III GEOGRAPHY
*Year 16 – 17 – 18*
1. Morphological mapping on small scale (breaks of slopes, angles etc.).
2. Morphological classification.
3. Hydrological system:
   (a) slope system (input, slope environment, output)
   (b) stream channel system
   (c) basin system.
4. Coastline system:
   (a) beaches: wind and waves, beach gradient, load, equilibrium, load movement;

(b) cliffs; sub-aerial and sea action on variable lithology and structure, slumping, mud flows, cliff falls;

(c) shoreline movement of water and load and resulting forms.

5. Glacial systems: accumulation and ablation of ice, movement of glaciers, glaciers as sources of water; ice-sheets

6. Periglacial systems: permafrost and seasonal permafrost; effect on water flow; processes of frost weathering, heave, solifluxion.

7. Geomorphological processes in arid areas.

8. Macro-scale changes: plate tectonics.

9. Problems of explanation in geomorphology.

## CLIMATIC SYSTEM

*STAGE III GEOGRAPHY*
*Year 16−17−18*

1. The atmosphere as a closed system
   (a) inputs of solar radiation, heat from land and sea, moisture — location of inputs.
   (b) outputs: radiation, heat and moisture — location of outputs.
   (c) the weather machine: transference of energy from tropical to polar regions; transformation of heat and potential energy to kinetic energy; the parameters of the atmosphere; temperature, pressure, winds and jet streams, relative humidity, their variation vertically and horizontally, their measurement and interpretation.
   (d) micro and meso-scale weather systems and their relation to climatic areas.

2. Short term and longer term changes in climate; problems of forecasting. Climate modification:
   (a) intentional
   (b) inadvertent

## BIOTIC SYSTEM

*STAGE III GEOGRAPHY*
*Year 16−17−18*

1. The ecological system as the interaction of inputs of heat and moisture with variables such as altitude, aspect, slope, drainage, soils and animals to produce vegetation:—

(a) measurement of the inputs and variables, and of the output by quadrat sampling
(b) mapping vegetation, analysis of plant communities and their development
(c) correlation of vegetation and soil pH values and soil moisture.

2. The pedological system: the interaction of inputs of heat and moisture, organic material and weathered rock to produce an output of soil particles, and water; measurement of soil variables air/water ratio, organic content, mineral content, texture, pH value, soil profiles.

3. Biotic systems on a macro-scale:
(a) Tropical forests: nature and extent — its stability — the effect of disturbing the system — soil erosion — secondary forest growth.
(b) Savanna — adaptation of plants, animals to climate — lateritic soil development.
(c) Desert vegetation and soils.
(d) Coniferous forest and tundra and their relationship to podsols.

4. Problems of man's interference with the biotic system.

## AGRICULTURAL SYSTEM

*STAGE III GEOGRAPHY*
*Year 16−17−18*

1. Detailed study of a farm as a system (inputs of heat, precipitation/irrigation water, fertilizer, labour; outputs of crops, animals; variables of soil, slope, aspect, techniques.)

2. Planning land use on a farm in relation to location of farmhouse and relief aspect and soil variables; farmers' perceptions.

3. Commercial farming in relation to Government economic policy. Costs-benefit analysis of changes in agricultural techniques.

4. Problems of:
(a) peasant and small scale farming in developed lands,
(b) peasant farming in developing countries,
(c) mono culture in developing countries.

5. Agricultural systems in relation to population growth and decline and to the ecosystem.

6. Agricultural land use patterns, historical and economic explanation — Uniform regions and agriculture.

7. Rural land use intensity and the friction of distance.

## MANUFACTURING SYSTEM

*STAGE III GEOGRAPHY*
*Year 16−17−18*

1. Classification of economic activity into primary, secondary, tertiary and quaternary, and the nature of manufacturing activity.
2. Detailed study of a manufacturing enterprise as a system (inputs, outputs, variables).
3. Distribution of manufacturing activity on:
   (a) macro-scale
   (b) meso-scale — the nature of this distribution.
4. Industrial location theory — Weber; optimizing and satisficing behaviour — chance factors.
5. The nature of industrial concentrations — linkages, economies of scale (internal and external) contrasts between older and newer industries in their location — the evolution of industrial regions. Multinational linkages.
6. Governmental policy on industrial location and distribution. Industrial location and environmental quality — a question of priorities.
7. Industrial growth and the depletion of raw materials and power resources.

## SETTLEMENT SYSTEM 1   POPULATION

*STAGE III GEOGRAPHY*
*Year 16−17−18*

1. Population data its sources and reliability — Problems of classifications of population (rural, urban, socio-economic group, ethnic group, etc.).
2. Population distribution on a macro and meso-scale.
3. Population growth — the exponential model — the demographic-transition model. Population growth and resources.
4. Population migration — mapping, explanation of migration, the socio-economic effects of migrations.
5. Rural depopulation and its effect on the regional system.

## SETTLEMENT SYSTEM 2   SETTLEMENT

*STAGE III GEOGRAPHY*
*Year 16−17−18*

1. Settlement patterns: concentration or dispersion; regularly or

randomly spaced; density decline; hierarchy of settlements according to size and function; rank size regularities, concepts of range, threshold and nesting.

2. Urban structure: functional zones, models of urban structure, the economic basis of zone differentiation, problems of twilight zones and urban ghettos. Concepts of bid-rent, density gradients.

3. Changes in urban population distribution, the decline of city centres and growth of suburban poles of attraction. Stress in the city.

4. The city and functional regions and relationship to administrative regions; growth centres and regional development; decision making on development; unplanned and planned development; the result of differential regional development.

5. Values and development in cities and regions; welfare versus efficiency.

6. Perception of urban areas; landmarks, paths, nodes, areas.

## SETTLEMENT SYSTEM 3   NETWORKS

*STAGE III GEOGRAPHY*
*Year 16–17–18*

1. Network geometry, vertices, edges; integration and connectivity; accessibility.

2. Flows along networks — their measurement and mapping; models explaining the extent of flow, e.g. gravity model.

3. The effect of transport networks on economic development, at the regional and national level.

4. Network growth historically and the changing values of different forms of communication; competition versus cooperation in transport at the city, region, national and international scales.

# CHAPTER FIVE

# Formulation of a Geography Course

## Introduction

The purpose of this chapter is to discuss ways in which the objectives chosen by a teacher may be married to content in order to provide geography courses for students of secondary schools. In Chapter 4 we examined some of the ways in which content might be derived from the ecosystem paradigm of geography, but no guidance was given as to how a course could be drafted, beyond giving some indication of the way individual items of content could be sequenced in terms of the age range of the students. Thus the content could be presented as a series of principles and concepts (Marsden 1976a) belonging to one or other aspect of the ecosystem paradigm, that is to geomorphology, climatology, agricultural systems and so on. Some means must now be found to articulate those concepts and principles into a course which will have coherence. It is important to note at the outset that there are many ways of doing this and no one method is necessarily better than another. Indeed, teachers will probably wish to experiment with different combinations of courses from time to time. In a dynamic situation courses will evolve as part of the curriculum process. I do not want, however, to exaggerate the extent to which this can be done. Clearly a measure of stability is important for both student and teachers who may be bewildered by a rapidly changing pattern of courses. Further the need to think out carefully how courses should be structured and to acquire appropriate resources will inevitably slow down the process of change. What ought not to happen is for a course to be developed and then remain unchanged for the next ten years. If this were to happen, the course would inevitably be left behind by events: ideas would have changed, the students would be different and the contextual examples would be out of date.

## Basic considerations: a case study

Let us assume that we are planning courses at the 'general level' as indicated in Chapter 3. The school may, in accordance with the recommendations of the *Taylor Report* (1977), have decided on its basic aims, that is what it is attempting to achieve as an institution with its pupils and students. These will probably be an elaboration in greater detail of what is stated at the top of the diagram in Figure 3.1 (page 43). The school curriculum planning committee (on which sit the heads of the departments) has agreed that modern geography is worth teaching because it helps to develop the mind, gives the student worthwhile knowledge and skills, as well as helping him, in common with other subjects, to develop social skills. However, the curriculum planning committee has stipulated that up to and including the third year of the secondary school, geography shall be included in a broad 'humanities' course which includes history, geography, social studies and religious education; and that thereafter geography shall be an optional subject. It has also been stated by the curriculum planning committee that the 'humanities' group shall be given three blocks of 1 hour 20 minutes on the timetable each week, and that geography in the fourth and fifth years should have two hours per week, either three single periods of 40 minutes each or a double period of 1 hour and 20 minutes, followed by a single period of 40 minutes. These timetabling considerations place certain constraints on the geography department's operations. Let us consider each part of the school course separately.

## Stage I Geography within a 'humanities course'

Clearly this will need to be planned in cooperation with teachers whose main concern is history, social sciences and religious education. The geographer needs to remember that some students will cease studying geography at the end of the third year course, consequently it is of some importance that many of the basic ideas and skills of geography should be included in the 'humanities' course. But it will be unreasonable to expect that the geographical component of the course will occupy more than one third of the total time. This calculation is based on the assumption that, social studies and religious education together will occupy about one third of the time. Let us further assume that each school year is 40 weeks long, but that owing to occasional holidays, interruptions to classes through examinations and special functions, only 36 weeks are really fully available. This means that geography can expect to be able to use one hour and 20 minutes for 36 weeks, or some other combination which would enable geography to use the same amount of time, such as four hours for 12 weeks. I am specifying 'geography – time' because I believe that only by allocating certain periods to the geographical elements of the 'humanities' course is it possible to ensure that geography will be taught. This does not imply that the 'humanities' course cannot be planned as an integrated course, but that the geographical viewpoint needs to come out clearly. In too many integrated courses, because no time is specifically devoted to particular elements, teachers spread themselves on historical or sociological aspects, and other elements in the course are all but ignored. Much may depend on who heads the curriculum planning team for the 'humanities' as Adams (1976) has pointed out.

The next step is decided on the basic unit of instruction. This might be a 'teaching unit' whose length may vary but which would essentially be concerned with attempting to achieve some relatively clear-cut, geographical objective. The choice of such teaching units would be based partly on the structure decided for the whole 'humanities' course and partly on the kind of geographical content deemed appropriate for students of the 11 – 14 age range as listed at the end of Chapter 4. Let us suppose that a 'humanities' curriculum adopted a series of themes such as community studies; living in towns; the family; population; evolution; early man; ancient civilization; work and industry; how people differ; other peoples and other cultures etc. (Lawton and Dufour 1973). Such topics are broad headings within which particular problems may be tackled and certain generalizations learned. If we take the first theme 'community studies', this seems to be a theme with a sociological slant in which the problem might be 'what do social scientists mean by a community?' which might be answered after examining the local community and perhaps some neighbouring ones. But, clearly, there is a spatial aspect to a community and this may be studied in an urban area by mapping residential property, according to a simple classification, such as 'terraced, semi-detached and detached houses' and discussing the characteristics of each area mapped and relating these to the socio-economic groups living in each area (see Settlement System Stage I, 11 – 12 years, in Chapter 4). The concept of community can legitimately be applied to plant communities and may be picked up again in the second year in the recognition of plant associations in such areas as heathlands and moorlands (see Biotic System Stage I, 12–13 years). Similarly, a topic like 'living in towns' can be looked at from an economic point of view, for example, by asking the question 'What do towns produce?', but it is clearly a suitable topic for considering geographical and historical questions, e.g. 'How did towns begin?' 'How have towns changed?' Thus, under the first questions some might consider how certain sites were selected and what environmental influences were at work, given the perceptions of those choosing the site (see Settlement Systems Stage I, 12–13 years).

There is therefore no great problem in incorporating a geographical element in a humanities course, granted the geographer in the team knows what he wants to teach. This is why I believe it important that the geographer should have available a list of concepts and principles such as that contained at the end of Chapter 4, to enable him to choose items which are appropriate both to the topic decided upon, and to the age group for which it is proposed. Even such a topic as 'the family', which may appear non-geographical, may be given a spatial aspect, since one of the characteristics of the modern family is its relative dispersion. Pupils may be asked to plot the locations of various members of their nuclear and extended families to indicate how clustered or dispersed they are and then analyse the reasons for this. Even the natural science aspects of geography, namely those which appear under the heading of climatic, geomorphic and biotic systems in the list in Chapter 4 may be incorporated under suitable headings. For example, the heading 'Work and Industry' may enable aspects of the agricultural system to be examined and its environmental influences (soil, climate, slope, aspect) while the heading 'Evolution' may make possible a consideration of the processes leading to change in the natural landscape and therefore of the geomorphic system.

Let us briefly return to the logistics of the operation. In Stage I of the secondary school course we assume that about 108 weeks (36 weeks per year) of school time will be available and that about 1 hour and 20 minutes per week will be used for the geographical aspect of the course. Now, since in the list of concepts and principles here are some 79 items, it follows that the operation is a feasible one. Some items will take more than one block of time on the timetable to deal with, for example, 'rocks as sources of raw materials and energy' (Geomorphic System 13–14 years), but others may take just one block of time or less, for example 'Variations in Air Temperature with

Altitude' (Climate System 12–13). In any case, just which items are included will be a matter for negotiation within the 'humanities' curriculum planning team.

## The geography teaching unit

What does a teaching unit consist of? Essentially a teaching unit consists of a statement of objectives followed by suggestions on how these objectives may be reached with the resources available and proposals for evaluating the unit. Much of a teacher's work involves the production of teaching units and their attempted implementation in the classroom. I write 'attempted implementation' advisedly as one can never be sure how a unit will work until it is tried out. Let us plan one teaching unit in relation to the 'humanities curriculum' – assuming the general theme is 'work and industry'. The social scientist may pose such questions as 'Why do people work? Is most work concerned with the satisfaction of basic needs?' (Lawton and Dufour 1973), the historian may ask 'How has industrial organisation evolved? How have the relationships between labour and management changed over the nineteenth and twentieth centuries?'. The geographer may ask 'Why is a particular factory situated where it is? Why has a certain group of industries developed in a port situation?'. It is useful to think in terms of a question which needs answering or of a problem to which a solution is sought. Thus the objective of a particular first year geography teaching unit might be 'to find out why light industry is often located in the suburbs of towns and along arterial roads.' It would be hoped that the students would come to understand that factories need relatively cheap but often extensive sites, that they need services such as gas, water, electricity and sewage, that they need transport close by, that they need a labour supply and that a suburban location near an arterial road tends therefore to be a suitable site. The next step is the finding of resources and the organisation of students' activities in order to direct their minds to answering the question posed. The whole teaching unit might be set out as follows:

## OBJECTIVE

To find out why light industry is often located in the suburbs of towns and along arterial roads.

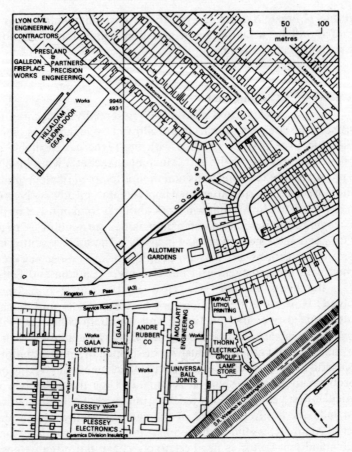

FIGURE 5.1. Industrial development on the Kingston by-pass.

## PROCEDURE

1. By oral questioning find out whether students understand what light industry is — clarify the notion by giving and asking for examples.
2. Ask students to examine large scale map showing the location of light industry along the A3 road in Kingston-upon-Thames (Figure 5.1) — Ask students to write down where the factories are found in the area mapped; and what area each factory covers compared with a house.

3. Get students to find out from a map of the London conurbation where Kingston-upon-Thames is situated (Figure 5.2).

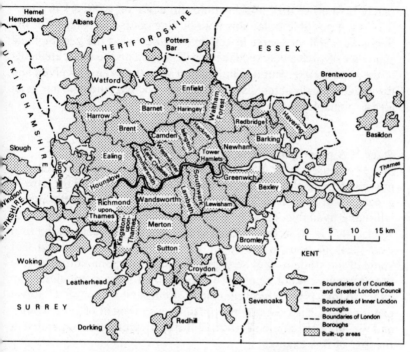

FIGURE 5.2. The growth of London and its administrative division.

4. Discuss with students why factories should be:
   (a) on outskirts of built up area;
   (b) near a main road;
   (c) not far from large housing estates;
5. Ask where else light industry may be found along a main road?
6. Conclude by asking students to write down the locational requirements of light industry.

This is a simple teaching unit requiring as resources two maps, both of which may be found in a current textbook (Graves & White 1978), and which probably requires between 40 and 80 minutes to complete, depending on the students and the extent to which the teacher makes the class write out its conclusions. It was a case study of industry along one section of the A3, to obtain a generalization about the location of light industry and the factors affecting this. Evaluation of this unit may be obtained by testing students on a similar map of, for example, the A4 road. The teacher will also find out how his students reacted, whether they appear to do the work set willingly or not.

It is not possible to lay down an outline course for Stage I of the Secondary School course in any detail, since what the geographical sequence of such a course may be, will depend on the other elements in the total course. But it is hoped that with the examples given and the geographical content list of Chapter 4, enough guidance has been given to enable such a course to be constructed.

### Stage II A geography course for ages 14 – 16 years

Since geography is available as a single subject on the timetable it is possible here to plan an outline which it is hoped will fulfil the aims of geographical education. The logistic assumptions are that the course will have available some two hours per week over a period of 68 weeks, that is 36 weeks in the fourth year and 32 weeks in the fifth year (examinations are in June). Further it must be assumed that some of the students will be sitting for external examinations whose requirements cannot be ignored. Consequently the curriculum plan which follows is for a two-year course aiming at the London 'O' Level examination. The course is preceded by a statement of general aims and the more specific objectives of the curriculum. It is appended at the end of this chapter.

In order to make each sub-heading relatively short, no attempt has been made to elaborate each into a statement of the principle or concept to be taught and learned. Nevertheless, the teacher will need to think out, in his planning of teaching units, just what it is he intends to teach. For example in the fourth year course, heading No. 2 (a) reads 'The Concept of a Cultural Landscape' and No. 2 (b) reads 'The Cultural Landscape Seen as a Product of Socio-economic Evolution'. Under No. 2 (a) what I have in mind is to communicate the idea that the landscape which we look at in rural areas is essentially a man-made landscape of farm buildings, hedges or fences, fields under various crops, roads, tracks, pylons and so on, and that such a landscape takes on different aspects in different cultural areas. Under 2(b) I want students to understand that cultural landscapes change over time in any one area as well as spatially between different areas. Sometimes the topic heading is very brief as in Topic No. 15 (c) Road and Rail. The suggested procedures usually give a clue as to what is intended. Here the problem to examine is, whether road and rail transport are competitors for a limited amount of traffic or whether they should be complementary; what are the economic and social environmental issues involved, in developing the road rather than the rail network, or in contracting the rail network?

An attempt has been made to order the course in some sequence and to group concepts and principles under topics which relate to one another. The suggested use of resources is based on currently available material but, clearly, will need to be changed as new resources become available.

Each teaching unit might be set out in some standard format as suggested below. Possibly this might be on a large card which might be available in the Geography Department for all members to consult. The cards could be brought up to date.

## TOPIC

*Example:* Man's use of rivers and river features (No.8 in Appendix).

## ESTIMATED TIME

Three periods of 40 minutes.

## OBJECTIVES

(a) Knowledge

*Examples:*

    (i)  to show that rivers may be used for irrigation, navigation, and power

    (ii)  to show that flood plains and deltas have competing land-uses

(b) Skills

*Example*

    the extraction of land use information from topographical or L.U. maps and its classification into broad categories

(c) Values

*Example:*

    to indicate that land-use decisions are based on values.

## LEVEL

Fourth Year CSE/GCE

## CONTEXT AND RESOURCES

*Example:* Lower Rhone Valley

C.G. Film Strip. The Languedoc development Scheme 1/50,000 maps of the Languedoc and Camargue.

I. B. Thompson – *The Lower Rhone and Marseille,* O.U.P., and maps and cards (see Curriculum Change or Classroom Survival by P. B. Thomas, *Geography*, vol. 63, January 1978). Questions on Work Cards.

## STRATEGIES

1. Use questions on work cards to establish use of Rhone river based on atlas search.
2. Find out land use of Languedoc and Camargue areas from filmstrip and topographical maps.
3. Discuss in small groups the nature of different land uses and which land-use type is increasing and why.
4. If the group controlled land use in the Camargue – what would they decide and why?

## EVALUATION

Teacher's evaluation of pupils' response to the unit
Teacher's assessment of course work produced.

### Summary and Conclusion

What has been attempted in this chapter has been no more than (1) to suggest procedures for formulating the geographical content of a humanities course for the first three years of a secondary school course and (2) to indicate a possible two-year course to 'O' level or C.S.E. for 15 and 16 year-old students in the normal, secondary, comprehensive school. Such courses have been based on the assumption that a loosely defined ecosystem paradigm of geography would be used. Clearly there is no compulsive reason why such a course should operate in any one school. Much will depend on local resources, talent and opportunities which arise. What I have done is to point to certain possibilities and certain sources of information. In many cases the reading indicated is more for the teacher than the students. In the ultimate analysis, whether the long-term aims of geographical education are achieved or not depends on the spirit in which the course is organised. Whether, for example, the students are encouraged to search for explanations through scientific enquiry rather than through authority. Whether they will come to question facile judgments or accept them. Whether they come to see situations as problematical or not. Whether they begin to look for systems in a mass of data. Whether they seek the spatial element in a problem. If they do, then their geographical education will have served some purpose and it will matter little whether they have forgotten particular facts or information that they had been taught during the courses which they followed.

From the teacher's point of view, devising a course is half the battle, but only half. The need to plan individual teaching units remains. It is in the skill with which these are designed that will to some extend ensure the success of the learning experiences that the students have. The feedback from the students with respect to teaching units is usually immediate or short term, consequently adjustments to such units can take place more frequently than adjustment to the whole structure of a course.

# Appendix to Chapter Five
## A Suggested Fourth and Fifth Year Geography Course
## To 'O' Level or C.S.E.

**Preamble**

This is an attempt at giving guidance on
(a)   the kinds of topics which might be included
(b)   the sorts of exercises which bring out the ideas and skills which it is intended the students should learn.

Although the language used is academic it is intended that the teacher should adapt both the language and exercises for the state of development that pupils have reached. The course is not meant for slow learners, though some of the ideas might prove useful.

Examples mainly from the British Isles and Europe are used, but it is not intended that this should be prescriptive. Teachers may use examples for which they have the necessary resources.

*The aims of geographical education are:*
1. To reinforce basic communications skills.
2. To develop spatial concepts.
3. To develop the ability to solve the spatial aspect of a problem.
4. To develop values relevant to environmental education.

*More specifically the objectives of this curriculum are:*
(cognitive, skill and attitudinal objectives)

1. To demonstrate that certain aspects of geographical knowledge are obtained through a physical science approach and others through a social science approach;
2. To show that physical factors have an important impact on the distribution of man-made features and therefore on human decisions;
3. To indicate that present spatial organisation patterns have evolved historically;
4. To bring out the kinds of processes (economic and social) which tend to produce regularities in the cultural landscape and those physical processes which produce regularities in the physical landscape;
5. To use a systems approach as a means of studying such physical systems as a river basin or weather system, and such socio-economic systems as a farming system;
6. To show how a systems approach may serve to integrate the physical and socio-economic aspects of certain problems;
7. To develop map drawing, map reading and other graphical skills;
8. To develop ability in the search for and use of geographical data.
9. To get students to demonstrate an interest in and concern for the environment at various scales;
10. To enable students to write clear reports on some of the problems studied.

**Evaluation**

It is expected that FORMATIVE EVALUATION will take place during the course through classroom feedback and short test and SUMMATIVE EVALUATION at the end of each year through:

(i)      assessment of course work presented,
(ii)     an objective type test,
(iii)    data response essay type questions.

**4th year**

| TOPIC | | SUGGESTED PROCEDURES |
|---|---|---|

1. *POPULATION*
   a. The distribution of population in Europe.

   a. Discussion of atlas maps of population density. Analysis of physical and economic factors affecting the distribution.

   b. Plotting population distribution.

   b. Drawing (a) choropleth (b) dot distribution, maps on prepared outlines from statistics, e.g. for English counties or French departments. Discuss advantages of each type.

   c. Sources of population data.

   c. Study photocopied pages of census of population statistics and require the extraction of certain information. Indicate secondary sources. Pose problem of reliability of information and size of enumeration area.

   d. (1) Comparison of rural and urban population densities.

   d. (1) Discuss (i) Limitations of overall population density maps.
   (ii) Problems of deciding whether population is urban or rural.
   Give figures of urban dwellers for several west, east and south European countries. Ask class to attempt to find reasons for differences from textbook.

   (2) Population movements.

   (2) Examine recent movements of population out of London and/or to Marseille and elucidate the push pull factors in migration (See King, R.; Bedford: the Italian Connection Geog. Mag., April 1977).

2. *RURAL LANDSCAPES*
   (a) The concept of a cultural landscape.

   2. (a) Analyse the elements of a landscape.
   (i) From field evidence in UK.
   (ii) From photographs of rural Belgium.
   Annotated field sketches to be drawn.

## 4th year contd.

| TOPIC | SUGGESTED PROCEDURES |
|---|---|
| (b) The cultural landscape seen as a product of socio-economic evolution. | (b) Study relevant passages extracted from Hoskins, *The Making of the English Landscape.* Use maps of villages in different stages of evolution. Students to write on what has changed since medieval times. What is currently changing in the British rural landscape. (See A. Glen, *The Scottish Environment*, Contemporary Scotland Series, Heinemann). |
| (c) Rural settlement patterns and village morphology. | (c) Use large and medium scale map evidence from UK and/or France and Germany to bring out dispersed and nucleated settlements. Students to produce sketch maps of:<br>(i) street and<br>(ii) compact villages<br>and indicate probable origin of differences. |
| 3. *PHYSICAL CONTRAINTS ON FARMING*<br>(a) The influence of slope aspect and altitude. | 3. (a) Case study of farms in Norway or Switzerland and vineyards in Rhône Valley. (See BBC programmes 'Europe from the Air'). |
| (b) The influence of temperature, total rainfall and rainfall régime. | (b) Use contrasting areas in northern, western, eastern and southern Europe to bring out climatic influences, e.g. dairying, arable grain farming, citrus fruit growing. How could an investor in farming minimize risks by owning farms all over the EEC? |
| (c) Chance factors. | (c) Students to take part in a farming game to bring out the influence of chance. |
| (d) Soils. | (d) (i) Case study of a single farm to show influence of soil on crop grown and yield.<br>(ii) Field study of soils to bring out influence of parent-rock, vegetation and climate; methods of classifying soils by structure and pH value. |

**4th year contd.**

| TOPIC | SUGGESTED PROCEDURES |
|---|---|
| **4. *RURAL ECONOMIES I*** <br> (a) The farm as a simple economic system. | 4. (a) Historical study of farmers reactions to price changes, e.g. in mixed farming economies contrasted with mono-culture economies. Use simple systems analysis to show input/output relations. Demonstrate that price rises may overcome physical constraints. Planning land use on a farm — Constructions of divided circles of land use on a farm. |
| (b) Government policy's influence on rural economies. | (b) Discuss and contrast <br> (i) collective farming and plan fulfilment <br> (ii) EEC farming policy (C.A.P.). |
| (c) The village in the rural economy. | (c) Contrast the functions of a village in an agrarian economy, e.g. in S. Italy, with those of a village in an industrial economy, e.g. U.K. |
| (d) Market towns and their sphere of influence. | (d) Use any available study of a market town e.g. Yvetôt in Normandy, Edam in Netherlands, to bring out functions of such towns. Use bus timeables or any other indices to get students to draw the sphere of influence of such a town. Discuss the idea of field of influence. |
| (e) The concept of a rural economy. | (e) Develop idea of an open system through diagrammatic representation of a rural economy. Students to draw their own diagrams of different rural economies. Revise subsistence economies by asking for a closed system representation. |
| **5. *RURAL ECONOMIES II*** <br> (a) Intensive and extensive farming. | 5. (a) Revise idea of extensive farming from study of North America and Australia—market gardening in Netherlands as an example of intensive farming—use a 1/35,000 map of the Polders to bring this out. (See Zwolle Sheet). |

**4th year contd.**

| TOPIC | SUGGESTED PROCEDURES |
|---|---|
| (b) Intensity of farming as a function of distance from urban centres. | (b) Use a LU map of an area near a large city. Students to indicate ways in which intensity decreases as distance from city increases. In what ways can this be measured? What factors are at work? Draw graph of land values and distance from city. |
| (c) Differences in rural land use on a national and continental scale. | (c) Revision of main physical constraints on farming by study of an overall land use map of France and/or Europe. Students to explain differences shown. What differences would a larger scale LU map indicate? |
| (d) Classification problems in agricultural land use—(multiple cropping, ley grass). | (d) Use LU map of Dutch Polders or Lower Rhône Valley. |
| 6. *THE PHYSICAL LANDSCAPE I* <br> (a) Scale differences in mountain areas. | 6. (a) Use 1/50,000 sheets of Alps and Grampians. Students to draw sketch maps and sketch sections from both sheets to bring out differences in size of features. |
| (b) Structural features. | (b) Study topographical maps, photographs and geological cross sections to bring out concepts of nappes and horsts and fault basins—inference from folds about mountain building process—concept of plate tectonics introduced (see 'The Restless Earth'). |
| (c) Revision of: <br> (i) Geological regularities. | (c) Case of Cornwall: <br> (i) Igneous cores, metamorphic aureoles, sedimentary peripheral areas; mineralization. (See Balchin, *Cornwall – British Landscapes through Maps, No. 9,* G.A.). |

**4th year contd.**

| TOPIC | SUGGESTED PROCEDURES |
|---|---|
| (ii) Features of glaciated mountains. | (ii) Topographical map study U-shaped valleys, corries, arêtes, horn descriptions to be given by annotated sketches. (Lake District Tourist Sheet, and Monkhouse, *The English Lake District – British Landscapes through Maps No. 1,* G.A.). |
| (iii) Features of a glacier. | (iii) Use photographs and an account of a mountaineering expedition to obtain descriptions of a glacier, its snout, crevasses, séracs, and lateral, medial and terminal moraines. |
| (iv) The evidence of glacial erosion and transport. | (iv) Photographic evidence of striation, documentary evidence of erratics, till, etc. used to demonstrate glacial erosion and transport. |
| (d) Man's use of high mountain areas. | (d) Use project approach—groups to develop displays relating to<br>(i) tourism<br>(ii) HEP<br>(iii) marginal farming in the Alps or Norway or Carpathians. |

## 7. THE PHYSICAL LANDSCAPE II

| TOPIC | SUGGESTED PROCEDURES |
|---|---|
| (a) Lowland physical landscapes in unglaciated areas of sedimentary rocks. | 7. (a) Use topographical map with geological tracing overlay on overhead projector to demonstrate relationships between rock type and physical features in scarpland areas — SE England or Paris Basin.<br>Geological sections to be labelled with appropriate terms: scarp face, back slope,. dip of rock, strike, joint, bedding planes. |

## 4th year contd.

| TOPIC | SUGGESTED PROCEDURES |
|---|---|
| (b) Lowland physical landscapes in 'Shield'. | (b) (i) Study of aerial photographs and/or 1/50,000 maps of Finland or Sweden or Canada to bring out lake and forest landscape — lumbering and pulp industries.<br>(ii) Documentary evidence of nature of rock basement and associated minerals — case study of Kiruna magnetite mines, Sweden (BBC TV). |
| (c) Lowland physical landscapes in areas of glacial deposition. | (c) Use generalized land use map of North European plain to bring out influences of physical factors: terminal moraines, outwash sands and gravels, urstromtaler, löss. Use generalized model of ice sheet retreat to demonstrate regularities in peri-glacial deposits. |
| 8. *RIVERS*<br>(a) The nature of water flow and its load. | 8. (a) Field work or secondary evidence used of the nature of (i) laminar (ii) turbulent flow. Use laboratory demonstration — demonstrate source of energy of flowing water; show that force exerted depends on mass as well as velocity. ($F = M \times A$) — factors influencing river load e.g. Isère river in France (See *Morisawa, Streams*, McGraw Hill 1968). |
| (b) The régime of a river and river drainage patterns. | (b) Use comparative figures for monthly flows of R. Seine and Loire (see *Labaste and Baleste La France*, Armand Colin) to show differences and infer from atlas reasons for differences. Effect on man's use of rivers. River drainage patterns (dendritic, trellised) in relation to land surface from 1/50,000 maps. |
| (c) The erosive and transport functions of rivers. | (c) Field work evidence to be used or laboratory experiments with sand and water. Landscape features as evidence of river's erosion: valleys, gorges. (See Film: 'Rivers at Work' M. Clark from N.A.V. Library and Granada T.V. 'The Dee', 'The Tweed'). |

**4th year contd.**

| TOPIC | SUGGESTED PROCEDURES |
|---|---|
| (d) The deposition of a river's load. | (d) Map and photographic evidence of braiding, slip off slopes, flood plains, terraces and deltas. (See *Sediments*, D. Briggs, Butterworth). |
| (e) Man's use of rivers and river features. | (e) (i) Study Languedoc irrigation development scheme (CG film strip).<br>(ii) The Rhine as an artery of trade — plot traffic flows on map — indicate nature of trade.<br>(iii) The Rhône delta's agricultural and tourist use, see 1/50,000 map or Michelin map.<br>(iv) What problems are caused by gravel exploitation in river valleys — use example Thames Valley (see Graves and White, *British Isles*, Heinemann). |
| (f) Floods. | (f) (i) Return to example of Loire to show how characteristics of river basin may lead to flooding. Students to draw two different river drainage systems, one likely to flood, the other unlikely.<br>(ii) Use contour map and ask students to indicate areas under water if depth of water were to rise to 3 metres above flood plain level.<br>(iii) With a river basin map ask for solutions to flood problem — contrast methods used by TVA. Man's perception of flood hazards. (See Newson, M. D. *Flooding and Flood Hazards in the UK*, OUP, 1975). (See Granada TV 'The Trent in the Land' Series). |

**4th year contd.**

| TOPIC | SUGGESTED PROCEDURES |
|---|---|
| 9. *COASTAL LANDSCAPES AND PROCESSES* <br> (a) Marine erosion in relation to rock type and rock structure; cove, headlands, arches, stacks at the local scale. | 9. (a) Use 1/50,000 map extracts of the Dorset Coast — or appropriate sheets of continental maps — e.g. 1/50,000 Etretat France. (See Clayton, K. 'Salvation from the Sea', *Geog. Mag.* July 1977) (Also 'The Lizard and Lands End, South Pembrokeshire', in *The Land* Series Granada TV). |
| (b) Structure in relation to changing sea levels. characteristics of submerged coasts; rias, fjords; general patterns of coastline at the regional level; concordant and discordant coasts. <br> (c) Advancing coastlines. | (b) Use an aerial photograph and maps of Cornish or Brittany coast for rias; W. Scottish or Norwegian Coast for Fjords; Dalmatian coast for concordant coastline and S.W. Ireland for a discordant coastline. <br> (c) Deltas (use Camargue); long shore drift (See Randall R. E., 'Shingle Street and the sea', *Geog. Mag.* June 1977); volcanic outflow (e.g. Iceland). Present evidence and attempted classification of advancing coasts. Try to obtain other examples. |
| 10. *WEATHER SYSTEMS* | 10. (Use T. J. Chandler's *Modern Meteorology and Climatology* as a resource for diagrams). |
| (a) Revision of weather types. | (a) Revision of weather types in the locality from direct observation. |
| (b) Air streams. | (b) Using the characteristics of the air of various weather types postulate the origins of air streams. Students to draw diagrammatic map of air stream movements over Europe. |
| (c) Simple mechanisms of the atmosphere. | (c) Using overhead projector transparencies of cross-sections of the atmosphere to illustrate: <br> Descending air and stability <br> Ascending air and instability <br> Concepts of convergence and divergence (use Met. office weather maps). <br> Weather systems revealed through the study of isobar maps — Anticyclone, depression. |

**4th year contd.**

| TOPIC | SUGGESTED PROCEDURES |
|---|---|
| (d) The depression. | (d) Weather sequence in a depression revealed by (i) sound film, or (ii) film loop. |
| (e) Exceptional weather. | (e) Using descriptive account bring out the effect of thunderstorms (Sept. 1970 S. England), long cold spells (Winter 1962/3); drought (1976). |
| 11. *NATURAL VEGETATION AND SOILS.* | 11. See E. M. Yates and R. Robson, 'A visit to Kew Gardens as Biogeographical Teaching', *Teaching Geography* No. 19. R. Mottershead 'Practical Biogeography', *Teaching Geography* Series No. 23. |
| (a) Relationship between soil, vegetation and climate. | (a) Use a case study of (i) a Mediterranean environment e.g. compare plant associations on limestone and crystalline rock hills of Provence (Estaque V. Maures hills: garrigues V. pines and eucalyptus + acacia) i.e. climate constant, soil and parent rock variable. (ii) compare limestone hills of Provence with limestone hills of East of Paris Basin (Estaque V. Plateau de Langres — garrigues V. mixed deciduous forest) i.e. similar parent rock but different climate). |
| (b) The ecosystem idea. | (b) Continue with garrigues as example summer drought → drought resisting vegetation (Aleppo pine, rosemary, thyme, cystus, juniper, holm oak) → small herbivores (rabbits, field mice, insects e.g. cicadas, birds e.g. partridge → carnivores (foxes, blackbirds, magpies) → students to develop a food web based on examples. |
| (c) Equilibrium and change in the ecosystem. The concepts of negative and positive feedback. | (c) Meaning of equilibrium. Factors making for change in the ecosystem e.g. a wet summer in the garrigues; a disease of pine trees; an exceptionally cold winter, an introduced new species of plant, myxamatosis. Use case of introduction of myxamatosis of France in the 1950s. |

## 4th year contd.

| TOPIC | SUGGESTED PROCEDURES |
|---|---|
| 12. *THE URBAN LANDSCAPE.* | 12. |
| (a) Revision of western man as an urban dweller. | (a) Draw bar graphs and proportional divided circles of the % of urban population in several European countries (see P. Hall, *World Cities*). |
| (b) The growth of a town. | (b) Evidence from the local town of the stages in its growth — evidence of house styles (see Cross and Daniels: Fieldwork) — see also Michelin guide for Paris — study historical evidence of complementarity between town growth and rural depopulation. |
| (c) Town morphology and functions. | (c) Revise functions of market town and examine concept of functional zones from map of London's (or any other large European city) main zones. Models of urban structure. Limitations of such models from a known local example. (see Graves and White, *British Isles*). |
| (d) The town economy. | (d) Examine occupational statistics for any large town and attempt classification into primary, secondary and tertiary — attempt to show which occupations might serve the town's needs only and which would serve a wider area — revise field of influence concept. |
| (e) New towns. | (e) Classify new towns according to reasons for their development in UK. (See Williams M., *New Towns* in *Contemporary Scotland Series*. Heinemann). |

**4th year contd.**

| TOPIC | SUGGESTED PROCEDURES |
|---|---|
| 13. *INDUSTRIAL LOCATION.* | |
| (a) The case of manufacturing industry. Industrial location and concentration. Linkages. | 13. (a) (i) Case studies of industrial location, e.g. Renault in Paris or Ford at Halewood to bring out siting factors. Elementary location theory in relation to Lackenby iron and steel works in Teesside. (ii) Case studies of industrial concentration — the external economies of scale, e.g. the Ruhr, or Donetz basin, (See also *Teaching Geography* No. 17 for the electricity generating industry). |
| (b) Ports as special cases. Port industries. | (b) Industrial concentration in port areas — e.g. Marseille — Fos (Resources from 'Port Autonome de Marseille') or Le Havre (See Tuppon J. N. 'Le Havre moves outwards', *Geog. Mag.* Nov. 1976). |
| (c) Decision making in industrial location. | (c) Use an industrial location game — e.g. iron and steel game (see 'Geography in Secondary Education'), Met. Fab. game — American High School geography project. |
| 14. *THE SPACING OF TOWNS.* | |
| (a) Distances between settlements of the same size. | 14. (a) Maps of towns with their sizes to bring out spacing regularities. |
| (b) The field of influence in relation to town size. The rank size rule. | (b) Blotting paper experiment to bring out field of influence idea — discussion of hierarchies of functions by comparing a village, a market town, a regional centre and a national centre — (See Graves and White, *British Isles*). Apply rank size rule to France, W. Germany and Italy and compare closeness of fit. |
| (c) The special case of a port's hinterland. | (c) The case of Le Havre or Hamburg. |

## 4th year contd.

| TOPIC | SUGGESTED PROCEDURES |
|---|---|
| 15. *INTERACTION BETWEEN TOWNS.* | |
| (a) Traffic flows approach to the gravity model. | 15. (a) Use field work or statistical evidence to show<br>(i) Traffic flows between two towns to be a function of their sizes and the distance between them<br>(ii) Distance decay (See *Teaching Geography* No. 14). |
| (b) The efficiency of a transport network. | (b) Exercises on the detour index, accessibility, $\beta$ index; time distance in relation to particular network (road, rail, air) (see *Teaching Geography,* No. 15). Estimate change in accessibility brought out by building of Humber Bridge or Bretonne Bridge on Seine. |
| (c) Road and rail. | (c) Draw comparative table of advantages of each method of transport for<br>(i) Goods<br>(ii) Passengers<br>Discuss cost problems for the infrastructure. (See Fullerton B, *The Development of British Transport Networks*, O.U.P., 1975). |
| (d) Air routes. | (d) Examine simple network of<br>(i) Domestic air routes<br>(ii) International air routes<br>to obtain factors influencing patterns. Look at timetables and case of London to New York Concorde flight to bring out influence of time zones.<br>Follow Flight from London to Tokyo (and return) to show influence of international date line. |
| (e) Airport locations. | (e) Use case of London's search for a third major airport, to bring out problems. (Graves and White in *British Isles*). Alternatively, study case of Charles de Gaulle airport for Paris. |

## 5th Year

In this year opportunities will be used to revise ideas and skills learned in previous years and comparisons will be made with other continents besides Europe — but most of the examples will be European.

| TOPIC | SUGGESTED PROCEDURES |
|---|---|
| 16. *POPULATION* <br><br> (a) Population growth in relation to crude birth and death rates; comparison between developed and developing world. | 16. (a) Use figures for <br>(i) West Germany <br>(ii) Nigeria <br>(See *Philip's Geographical Digest*). |
| (b) Elementary consideration of the demographic transition model. | (b) Case of Mauritius (See *American High School Geography Project*). |
| (c) The concept of overpopulation in relation to economic development and resources. | (c) Compare the economy of India and that of the UK. What are the structural differences in terms of numbers in the primary, secondary and tertiary section of the economy (See CWDE[1] materials: Haywood, 'Altiplano Life'; *Teaching Geography* Vol. 1 No. 5, 1976). Discuss question of whether Britain is overpopulated compared with France. |
| (d) Population migration and ethnic minorities. | (d) Examine case of UK or France or Germany: <br>(i) Nature and location of ethnic minorities <br>(ii) Reasons for immigration (push/pull factors) <br>(iii) Problems resulting from migration e.g. West Indians in UK; Algerians in France, Turks in Germany. |
| 17. *AGRICULTURAL SYSTEMS* <br><br> (a) Farmer's perceptions of their environment. | 17. (a) Case of immigrant farmer in Southern France or Corsica coming from Algeria — Alternatively, use American High School Geography Project Materials — Farming as a way of life for peasant communities. |
| (b) Cultural variations in attitudes of farming. | (b) Compare a commercial farm in Polders with a peasant holding in Southern Italy (See 'Europe from the Air' BBC TV). |

[1] CWDE = Centre for World Development Education

**5th year contd.**

| TOPIC | SUGGESTED PROCEDURES |
|---|---|
| (c) Environmental Pollution and commercial farming — disturbances of an ecosystem | (c) Revise ecosystem notion by considering case of nitrates being used as fertilizers to raise yields of cereals but nitrates drain into local rivers, cause excessive growth of aquatic plants. |
| (d) The farming system as part of the total economic system. | (d) (i) Consider effect on farming system of growth and development of an economy e.g. France in post war years — rural depopulation, abandoned farms, increasing size of holdings.<br>(ii) Government policies and farming — The Common Agricultural Policies in Europe — Use table to show objectives of C A P in relation to various means of achieving these objectives — Debate: Dear or cheap food policies? |
| (e) Classification of farming types. | (e) Revision of types of farming to be found in the world:<br>Subsistence farming:<br>  i. shifting cultivation<br>  ii. sedentary<br>  iii. nomadic pastoralism<br>Commercial farming:<br>  i. plantations<br>  ii. extensive<br>  iii. intensive<br>  iv. horticulture<br>Present cases and make students clarify them (See Highsmith *Case Studies in Human Geography*, also Association of Agriculture sample farms, also Glen, A., *Farming in Contemporary Scotland* Series, Heinemann). |
| 18. *THE BIOTIC SYSTEM*<br>(a) Plans successions and the concept of a climax vegetation. | 18. (a) Use study of a particular plant succession e.g. on a patch of waste ground — See 'Schematic treatment', in Haggett, *Geography a Modern Synthesis* — The Natural Vegetation belts as examples of steady state climax vegetations — |

**5th year contd.**

| TOPIC | SUGGESTED PROCEDURES |
|---|---|
| (b) Man's influence on plant communities: disturbing the ecosystem. | (b) (i) The effect of catastrophes e.g. fire — on climax vegetation — the concept of secondary growth e.g. in Mediterranean pine forests devastated by fire.<br>(ii) Lumbering — reafforestation e.g. Forestry Commission Forests in Britain, Pacific Coast Forest in British Columbia (See 'Dinkele, Plana forest', *Teaching Geography* vol. 1, No. 3, 1976)<br>(iii) Overgrazing in developing countries e.g. in Ethiopia and Somalia, Kenya (See Whiting, 'Karimojong', *Teaching Geography* vol. 1, no. 5, 1976). |
| (c) Man's influence on soils: the need for conservation. | (c) (i) Monoculture, soil impoverishment and erosion; attempts to counter this with inorganic and organic fertilizers —<br>(ii) Soil conservation practices, the example of the USA (For general reference see Simmons I.G. *The Ecology of Natural Resources*, Arnold 1974). |

19. *THE PHYSICAL LANDSCAPE*

| TOPIC | SUGGESTED PROCEDURES |
|---|---|
| (a) Classification of macro — relief features into:<br>(i) Lowland sedimentary areas<br>(ii) Alpine type mountains<br>(iii) Block mountains<br>(iv) Volcanic features | 19. (a) Use relief map of Europe, get students to complete a table giving examples in each category. |
| (b) Revision of main rock types<br>(i) Sedimentary<br>(ii) Igneous<br>(iii) Metamorphic | (b) Use photographs of landscapes representing each type and samples of rocks of each category — students to allocate rock type to each landscape — students to describe the physical characteristics of each type. |

## 5th year contd.

| TOPIC | SUGGESTED PROCEDURES |
|---|---|
| (c) The hydrological cycle in a drainage basin. | (c) Students to draw a systems diagram of a drainage basin showing the various components which interact in the hydrological cycle (see *Classroom Geographer*, Front Cover, October 1977, Weyman D. R., *Run Off Processes and Stream Flow Modelling*, O.U.P. 1975 and 'Hydrology for Schools', *Teaching Geography No. 25*, G.A., 1975). |
| (d) Landscape evolution and the idea of dynamic equilibrium at the meso scale. | (d) Study of a receding cliff in chalk as an example of morphological stability within a dynamic system — The free face constant slope morphology of certain cuestas as examples of such dynamic equilibrium — Analogy with a stationary glacier. (See Small, 'The new geomorphology and the sixth former', *Geography* vol. 54, 1969; Clark, Ricketts and Small; 'Barton does not rule the Waves' *Geog. Mag.*, July 1976). |
| (e) Landscape evolution at the macro scale — mountain building and plate tectonics classification of past earth movements into Caledonian, Hercinian and Alpine. | (e) Examination of regularities in the recent mountain chains, island areas and ocean deep — Association of mountain chains with volcanicity and earthquakes — Explanation in terms of plate movements (See Nigel Calder — *The Restless Earth* BBC, also BBC Filmstrip on plate tectonics) — Examination of older mountains in Norway, France and Scotland — Division into the Caledonian and Hercinian system according to trend. cf. N. America. |
| (f) Glacial and periglacial landscapes. | (f) Use examples of Alps and/or Himalayas to distinguish between landscapes subjected to glacial erosion and those subjected to fluvial action under periglacial conditions — Case studies in the Alps and Provence with 1/50,000 maps to illustrate differences. Students to complete a table to give four examples of each landscape. |

**5th year contd.**

| TOPIC | SUGGESTED PROCEDURES |
|---|---|
| 20. *CLIMATIC SYSTEMS*<br>(a) The idea of climatic classification. | 20. (a) (i) Students to analyse the elements which enable the categorization of a climate e.g. the North West European or West Coast cool temperate type.<br>(ii) Students to suggest the main considerations which enable geographers to classify climates.<br>(iii) Students to attempt to complete a world map divided into climatic types, indicating the characteristic of each area based on climatic data (Mean monthly temp. and mean monthly rainfall and rainfall régime). |
| (b) The atmosphere as a closed system. An elementary model of the general circulation — The transference of heat polewards. | (b) (i) Relate Equatorial climate, hot desert and tropical continental climate to the Hadley cell and excess heat intake at equator<br>(ii) Relate Mediterranean climate to alternate influence of Hadley cell in summer and depressions in winter<br>(iii) Relate North-West European climate to the zonal circulation and depression systems.  •<br>(iv) Relate Polar and Cold temperate climates to heat loss areas of polar regions. (See T. J. Chandler *Modern Meteorology and Climatology*, Chandler and Musk, 'The atmosphere in perpetual motion', *Geog. Mag.* Nov. 1976). Use overhead projector transparencies of the parts of the model. |

## 5th Year

| TOPIC | SUGGESTED PROCEDURES |
|---|---|

**21. *THE MANUFACTURING SYSTEM***

(a) The distribution of industry within the UK.

21. (a) Use thematic maps showing the distribution of industry — to indicate the broad pattern (e.g. as in *Readers Digest Atlas*).

(b) The location quotient as an index of regional specialisation.

(b) Case study of South Wales to show how the location quotient is calculated. Ask students for its limitations.

(c) Industrial location and land-use conflicts.

(c) The case of nuclear power stations.

(d) Government policy with respect to industrial location.

(d) The development area policy in the UK. The case of N.E. England (For (a), (b), (c) and (d) See Graves and White, *British Isles*).

(e) Pollution and industrial location.

(e) (i) The case of the Rhine — Discussion of documentary. (See Shell film. The river must live').

(ii) Air pollution — Smokeless zones in Britain and the case of brick and cement works.

(iii) Radioactive wastes. (The Windscale enquiry 1978).

**22. *THE SETTLEMENT SYSTEM***

(a) Urban growth compared in the developed and developing world.

22. (a) Examine growth of Zurich ('Europe from the Air', BBC TV) and Calcutta (*Geographical Magazine*, October 1968).

(b) Urban renewal.

(b) The case of Birmingham (See Graves and White, *British Isles*), or Leeds (See Dickinson and Shaw, 'Coronation Street moves out of town', *Geog. Mag.* Feb. 1977).

(c) Land-use conflicts in urban areas.

(c) Offices versus residential accommodation in London (See GYSL Project).

(d) Urban dwellers' perceptions of town.

(d) Use experiment with students — what features strike them as noticeable in their locality (See Gould and White *Mental Maps*, Penguin, 1974).

**5th year contd.**

| TOPIC | | SUGGESTED PROCEDURES |
|---|---|---|
| (e) The city region concept and administrative divisions. | (e) | The British administrative county and the planning region examined as exemplars of the city region (See Hall, P., *Urban and Regional Planning*, Penguin, 1974 and Davies, R. L. *Marketing Geography*, Metheun 1976). |
| (f) Urban quality. | (f) | Students to rate known streets and areas for environmental quality — Discussion of characteristics which make for urban quality (See Street Work, The Exploding School, Fyson and Ward, Longmans) also Arvill, *Man and Environment*, Penguin 1967). |
| (g) Ethnic conflict in cities. | (g) | The case of Belfast, (See Boal, F. W., Murray, R. C. 'A city in conflict', *Geog. Mag.* March 1977). |
| 23. *NETWORKS AND COMMUNICATIONS AND REGIONAL BALANCE* | | |
| (a) Urban road traffic: a special case of land use conflict. | 23. (a) | Study of the case of Birmingham (Graves and White, *The British Isles*). The conflict between traffic flow and environmental quality. |
| (b) The National Network in relation to regional planning. | (b) | The motorway network in Britain in relation to regional development, Comparisons with France and Germany — why is there no completed motorway to the channel port? (See *Teaching Geography* No. 26 E. Rawling, 'Motorway'). |
| (c) The concept of a trade network. | (c) | The distance decay principle in relation to the trading partners of the UK. (See *Annual Abstract of Statistics*). |
| (d) Trade and regional imbalance. | (d) | The Mezzo-giorno and the Ruhr within EEC. A study in contrasts — use of comparative table. |
| (e) Trade and political groups. | (e) | The spatial manifestations of political groups — EEC, COMECON, GATT. |

# CHAPTER SIX

# The Sixth-Form Course
# (16–19 years)

## Introduction

The sixth-form course is likely to be somewhat different from previous courses in that students will be those voluntarily staying on at school in order to gain further knowledge and experience as well as qualifications. Traditionally, those staying on in the sixth form were students intending to sit for the 'A' level examination, with a view to going on to higher education or in order to obtain a qualification and secure entry into a job requiring a higher standard than that afforded by an 'O' level G.C.E. Certificate. In 1975, some 28 per cent of first-year sixth formers and 18 per cent of all sixth formers were on courses other than 'A' level (Schools Council 1978a). Consequently the sixth-form is no longer homogeneous, neither is its population largely to be found in schools. The students studying geography in the 16–19 age group may be found in schools, sixth-form colleges, tertiary colleges and colleges of further education (Taylor *et al* 1974). The purpose of this chapter will be to examine the special nature of curriculum planning problems for geography in the sixth form and to outline certain provisional suggestions. As indicated later (in Chapter 7), a Schools Council curriculum development project (Geography 16–19) is currently considering the geography curriculum for the age group; and will complete its allotted task in the summer of 1982.

## The Background

Bearing in mind the elements of the curriculum process outlines in Chapter I (Figure 1.3), it seems clear that the geography curriculum in the sixth form will result from the interaction of the (1) aims set by society and the school, the aims and objectives derived from the subject, and the aims of the students; (2) the changing nature of the content of geography; (3) the kinds of learning experiences provided by teachers and (4) the nature of the evaluation procedures used.

Let us take one aspect at a time. First the aims set by society and the school and those derived from geography. Ever since the Crowther report (1959), there has been a move to widen the sixth-form curriculum as a whole. In effect, society is requiring (through its educational institutions) its 18 and 19 year-old students to leave school and college with a broader, less specialised knowledge than has been the case hitherto. Hence the current Schools Council proposals to widen the traditional sixth-form curriculum to five subjects. We shall look at the details as they affect geography in the next section. But those who study in the sixth form without intending to follow a 'traditional' course are also expected to widen their perspectives, though the criterion of relevance to working life is often used in relation to such non-traditional courses. Within the subject itself, values have shifted towards those emphasizing scientific enquiry, environmental issues and spatial organisation. It is in the sixth form that most students may find themselves beginning to appreciate more fully what is meant by hypothesis testing, value clashes in environmental quality and town planning.

Secondly, the content of the subject has changed and is continuing to change. The emphasis is moving away from regional studies to systematic or thematic studies within an overall paradigm of the spatial organisations or ecosystem type. In so far as sixth form curriculum is closer to curricula in higher education than the lower school curriculum, it follows that developments in the content of geography which are currently resulting in a growth, for example, of perception studies and the geography of welfare, may soon be reflected in the sixth form. Thus pressure is exerted to modify the content used in curricula to take into account new research findings and new techniques of analysis. The use of phenomelogical approaches is increasingly being suggested to complement the logical positivistic approaches more generally used (Ley 1977). Thirdly, as in the lower school, the kinds of teaching strategies used by teachers are being widened in scope, though it would be wrong to suggest that there was a widespread distribution of the more elaborate teaching techniques. But the use of individual study assignments and group enquiry are increasing and the lecture note-taking technique is probably decreasing.

Fourthly, the evaluation methods used are now more numerous than they once were. Besides the traditional essay questions, evaluation may involve the assessment of an individual study, of course works, of objective test questions, of field work and an oral test. To some extent those changes are already evident in the syllabuses published by the G.C.E. examination boards for example, the Joint Matriculation Board's 'A' level syllabus which gives a choice between a project and a practical examination as well as traditional written papers. Inevitably these lag considerably behind the events which are currently influencing teachers of geography. Most G.C.E. boards have produced new syllabuses for geography at 'A' level in the past 10 years. For example, a new University of London 'A' level syllabus was first examined in the Summer of 1978, though it was first published some years prior to that date to give teachers an opportunity to prepare for it. The G.C.E. boards have also taken notice of the tendency for some sixth formers to require a one-year course in the sixth form which is different from the traditional 'O' level course. The alternative 'O' level syllabuses provide this need. Similarly, the C.S.E. boards have provided experimental syllabuses for the Certificate of Extended Education (C.E.E.) courses which have been tried out in various institutions.

## The problem of a five-subject curriculum

The proposals to widen the sixth-form curriculum have had a long and chequered history dating back to the 1950s. Although the Crowther report reaffirmed the concept of study in depth in the sixth form, it tempered this by suggesting minority time to be spent by students in studying subjects other than those in which they were to be examined. Not long after the Crowther report many suggestions were made to establish more firmly a much broader curriculum. After many still-born proposals, the Schools Council eventually published the suggestions contained in Working Papers, Numbers 45, 46 and 47 (1972, 1973a and b). These indicated the nature of broad curricula and the examination structure to support them. The proposals are that the present three-subject 'A' level curriculum be replaced by a five-subject curriculum, but that of the five subjects, three be studied at what is called Normal or 'N' level and two at Further or 'F' level. The distinction between 'N' level and 'F' level was originally indicated to be in terms of the time devoted to subjects at each level. Subjects taken at 'N' level would normally take up half of existing 'A' level time on the curriculum and subjects studied to 'F' level would take up approximately three quarters of the time devoted to an 'A' level subject. The aim was to squeeze five unequal subjects into the time taken by three equal subjects, i.e. – three 'A' levels = $(3 \times \frac{A}{2}) + (2 \times \frac{3A}{4})$. The rationale behind the difference between 'N' and 'F' level subjects was that the curriculum would be broadened, but that students wishing to pursue subjects in higher education would have an opportunity to study at least two subjects in great depth. The 'N' and 'F' level proposals must be seen as a compromise between those who wanted to broaden the curriculum and those, like the Standing Conference on University Entrance, who felt that students could not follow a three-year, university, honours degree course unless their pre-university course had brought their knowledge up to a level roughly equivalent to the 'A' level examination. It is perhaps also a position taken by university authorities in the light of the unlikelihood of university honours courses being extended to four years. It ought perhaps to be recorded that the Association of University Teachers (AUT) took a different view; it saw the need for a broader curriculum, but felt that the differentiation between 'N' and 'F' level subjects was an unnecessary complication, a view with which I have much sympathy. I have outlined elsewhere the problems of 'N' and 'F' for geography in terms of the distinctions to be made between the two levels. (Graves 1977). I will briefly summarise the position as I see it. Clearly if the 'F' level simply means covering a broader content, no problem arises. But if as the Standing Conference on University Entrance insists, 'F' level must be conceptually more difficult than 'N' level, then this does pose a problem for geography bearing in mind that the difference between the two courses is only one of one quarter of the time normally devoted to 'A' level subjects. That is if 'F' level students get three hours teaching per week in each year of the sixth form, then 'N' level students will get two hours – whether this difference will in reality mean that 'F' level students are conceptually more advanced than 'N' level students is difficult to affirm, given the wide variations in student performance. It is also difficult to spell out what this difference means in terms of curriculum and of evaluation. Strictly, 'F' level questions ought to be more difficult than 'N' level questions.

The Schools Council set up a Geography Syllabus Steering Group to report to the Joint Examinations Sub-Committee (JESC) of the Schools Council on the feasibility of the 'N' and 'F' proposals for geography. After commissioning three separate groups to put forward proposals for an 'N' and 'F' curriculum in geography, the Geography Syllabus Steering Group, consisting of teachers in secondary, further and higher education, reported back on the feasibility of the proposals to JESC. This report contains the suggestions of the three commissioned groups (Schools Council 1977b).

It is not easy to summarize the reports of each group and those wishing detailed information must read them in full. Broadly, the first group, based on the Geographical Association, produced two specimen syllabuses, based on the idea of a common syllabus for 'N' and 'F' students. In the first syllabus, the distinction between 'N' and 'F' students lies in the somewhat greater content coverage of 'F' level students, whilst in the second specimen syllabus, the content coverage is the same for 'N' and 'F' students, but the latter are expected to cover the content in greater depth. The second commissioned group was based on the Oxford and Cambridge Schools Examination Board. It produced suggestions for a differentiated 'N' and 'F' level curriculum, in which the 'F' level was supplementary to the 'N' level and at a higher intellectual level. These differences are spelt out in great detail in the report which is full of useful suggestions, though the Syllabus Steering Group had some doubts about the feasibility of teaching either the 'N' or 'F' syllabuses in the time available. A feature of the syllabus was its division into spatial awareness, regional awareness and environmental awareness.

The third Commissioned Group, based on the West Midlands Geography Teachers' Group produced a modular curriculum for 'N' and 'F' level. The principles on which this curriculum is based are the following:

(1). The 'N' and 'F' courses are based on modules, i.e. sections of courses, lasting 12 weeks or approximately one term.

(2). 'N' level students are to complete five modules and 'F' level students seven modules in the two years of the course.

(3). Progression intellectually is ensured by having three levels of modules; level 1 modules provide a foundation course for both 'N' and 'F' level students; level 2 modules are more difficult and offer an intellectually rewarding course for 'N' level students; level 3 modules are more difficult still and designed for

'F' level students only. Thus 'N' level students would take two level 1 modules and three level 2 modules, whilst 'F' level students would take two level 1, three level 2 and two level 3 modules.

The examples of modules are given in Figure 6.1.

FIGURE 6.1.

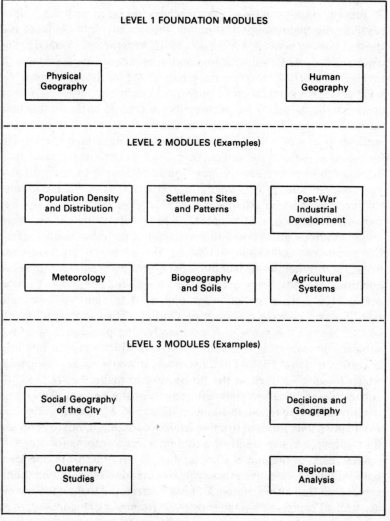

*Source:* Schools Council 1977(a)

All three commissioned groups suggested that assessment should be partly by examination and partly by course work assessment. Further discussion of the 'N' and 'F' proposals for geography may be found in Frey (1978) and Grenyer (1978).

## The present situation

At present sixth-form geography teachers are faced with the task of teaching two main groups of students, those studying at 'A' level and those following non- 'A' level courses. If the Schools' Council proposals are accepted, then teachers may find themselves teaching at 4 levels, 'N' level, 'F' level, and a group sitting for the alternative 'O' level or CEE examination or even no examination at all. It seems clear that the 'N' and 'F' level students are likely to be taught together in the first year, but separately in the second year. The one-year students (i.e. the 'A'/'O', CEE and non-examination students) will be taught separately. Consequently, a geography department in a large comprehensive school may find itself having to teach in any year: one 'N' and 'F' first-year group; one 'A'/'O', CEE group, one 'N' level second-year group and one 'F' level second-year group, i.e. four separate groups of students, where before only three were taught. Various other possibilities exist, but the other main suggestion which may economise on time, is that 'N' and 'F' level students be taught together for most of the second-year programme, with some additional periods being given to 'F' level students only. Thus at present (1978) teachers of geography need to plan 'A' level and non-'A' level courses based on recently modified examination syllabuses and at the same time prepare for the possibility of a five subject curriculum at 'N' and 'F' levels, which may be put into operation in 1984! In the circumstances, it would seem reasonable, whilst looking forward to the future, not to make the 'N' and 'F' curriculum in geography so different from the new 'A' level curriculum as to give teachers an impossible task. My own predilection would be to look forward to a five subject curriculum, but to abandon the two levels; consequently the content which I propose for Stage III (16–18 years) at the end of Chapter 4 is set out in terms of one level only. Similarly, because most syllabuses tend to over-extend themselves (see Hall 1976 Chapter 5), I have attempted to limit the coverage whilst keeping within the ecosystem framework (Figure 4.4, page 68).

## Some suggestions

The curriculum planning models at the general and at the instructional levels proposed in Chapter 3 will apply to the 16–18 or 19 course, as they did to the 11–16 course. The difference will lie in the greater influence of the evaluation technique used, since all sixth-form courses are only one or at most two years away from the ultimate assessment. Consequently, it is important that the nature of the examination be appropriate. I would suggest in the first place that the 'A' or 'N'/'F' level courses be examined on the basis of 25% of the marks being given to course work and 75% to examination work, but that in 'O'/'A' and CEE courses the ratio be 50% for external examination. The rationale behind such a suggestion lies in the reluctance of many teachers to be too involved in course work assessment at 'A' level, and in the recognition that for some one-year course students, too great a reliance on formal externally examined work gives an inadequate impression of their performance.

In the second place, I would argue that the externally examined section of the assessment should be made up of (i) an objective test, (ii) structured data response questions and (iii) essay questions. This is in response to the fact that each form of examination tests somewhat different abilities and candidates should therefore be asked to perform on all three forms. It will be objected that reliable objective tests in geography do not exist at 'A' level (or equivalent). This is true for the United Kingdom, but the Australians have used such tests and it is not beyond the wit of research units in Universities or University Examinations Boards to develop such tests, though this would take time. The internally examined element could be in the form of course work, a special local study and/or field work.

In the third place, it is necessary that the examinations boards be modest in their content requirements. This may be done either by considerably restricting the content covered or by allowing candidates or schools to choose elements or modules within a wider content area. If it be important that students use enquiry methods and examine a topic in depth, then some limitation of total coverage must occur. In any event, candidates and teachers limit their study to what is possible in the time available by the traditional question spotting technique, which occasionally goes disastrously wrong! To some extent this need to limit the content covered is beginning to be recognised by examinations boards. The alternative ordinary ('A'/'O') level examination in geography of the University of London

School Examinations Board gives the candidate a choice of two out of eight among the following topics: cartography and surveying; landforms, landscapes and life; meteorology, climatology and biogeography; land and resources in present-day Britain; the geography of towns and settlements; industrial location; historical geography; agricultural geography.

For the present an 'A' level course often has eight 40-minute (or 4 × 80 minutes) periods allocated to it, giving a total over five terms of (8 periods × 12 weeks per term × 5 terms) 480 periods. On this basis an 'N' level course would have 240 periods and 'F' level course 360 periods. In practice the 'N' and 'F' level courses might be a little longer as the very existence of a five-subject curriculum would lessen the need for minority time which was built into the traditional 'A' level timetable. In terms of the content outlines at the end of Chapter 4 for the 16–18+ age group, I would argue that the traditional 'A' level course could cover most of the items listed, though some would be studied at greater depth than others. All items are not, in any case, equivalent with each other in terms of time required to cover them adequately. An 'N' level course could clearly cover only half the items, and I would suggest to ensure flexibility that out of the six elements (geomorphic system; climatic system; biotic system; agricultural system; manufacturing system; settlement system) students be allowed to choose three, granted that one is within natural systems and one within the man-made, systems group. An 'F' level course could be organized on the basis of four elements, again on the understanding that at least one element must be chosen from the natural systems and one from the man-made systems. The greater amount of time available would allow 'F' level students to delve somewhat deeper into each element chosen. How much choice students may in fact have must depend on the teacher and other resources of the geography department concerned.


### An example

Assuming the logistic problems of how much time to give to each course have been solved, given the manpower available, let us look at the organisation of a typical teaching module. The 'settlement system' element will provide the example. Within this element there are sub-sections dealing with (i) population, (ii) settlement patterns and (iii) networks. I propose to use the population sub-section. The term module is used to indicate a group of teaching periods which form a unit.

## POPULATION

### GENERAL AIMS
To make students aware of the nature of population growth and distribution problems and of ways of studying these problems scientifically.

### SPECIFIC OBJECTIVES
A. Knowledge
1. To find out the sources of population data and their reliability.
2. To understand the concepts of crude birth-rate, crude death-rate, general fertility-rate, annual rate of growth of population.
3. To be aware of the necessarily arbitrary nature of classification schemes for rural/urban population, for socio/economic groups, for ethnic groups.
4. To realise that population distribution patterns vary with the scale at which they are examined.
5. To be aware of the demographic transition model of population growth and of its applicability or non-applicability to various countries.
6. To understand the complexity of the relationship between population, natural resources and standard of living.
7. To be able to classify population migration:
   (i) spatially into: (a) intra-regional; (b) inter-regional; (c) international migration;
   (ii) temporally into: (a) daily; (b) seasonal; (c) permanent migration.
8. To understand that permanent migration occurs because of combinations of 'push-pull' forces.
9. To be aware of the special effect of migration from rural to urban areas on the regional economics of (a) developed countries (b) developing countries.

B. Skills
1. To be able to look up population data from statistical year books and census digests.
2. To be able to map population distributions using dot techniques choropleth, isopleths, proportional divided circles (some of this

    may have been taught in the lower school), at different scales; drawing population pyramids.

  3. To be able to apply the exponential growth model ($N_t = N_o e^{rt}$) to predict population growth.

  4. To be able to map population migrations by flow diagrams.

C. Values

  1. That classification of populations into socio-economic or ethnic groups does not imply the superiority or inferiority of any one group.

  2. That the material well-being of one population compared with another does not imply the superiority, in any other sense, of the population with the higher standard of living.

  3. That unchecked population growth is not a desirable state in any country.

  4. That attempts should be made to husband resources, because of their finite nature and the present tendency for world population growth.

N.B. Knowledge, skill and value objectives are separated out for analysis, but they will by taught together in practice.

*TIME AVAILABLE*

10 periods – N.B. Some work will be done outside formal teaching time i.e. during private study periods and for homework.

*SUGGESTED PROCEDURES*

**Period 1** (40 mins.)

(a) Expository teaching on sources of population data.

*Sources:* Various statistical year books

(b) Discussion of factors making for reliability or unreliability.

(c) Exercise on extracting population data from *Annual Abstract of Statistics, Statesman's Year-Book. U.N. Statistical Year-Book, Europa Year-Book.*

**Period 2**
*Source:*
(a) *Philips Geographical Digest*

(b) Bradford & Kent *Human Geography* O.U.P.

(a) Exercise comparing crude birth and death-rates for developed and developing countries to show countries in the different stages of the demographic transition model.

(b) Discussion of the demographic transition model's applicability to different countries over time.

**Period 3**
*Source:* Haggett
*Geography – a modern synthesis,* Harper and Row

Predicting population growth.
(a) Drawing a population pyramid from data
(b) Expository teaching of the exponential growth model (including annual growth rate).
(c) Exercises to predict the population in the year 2000 of UK, W. Germany, USSR, India, China.

**Period 4**
*Sources: Statesman's Year Book;* Graves (Ed.) Teaching materials on population international understanding and environmental education — Unesco

(a) Case studies of (i) India or Philippines (ii) W. Germany; from point of view of population pressure on resources — The difficulty of the concept of over-population in relation to standard of living.
(b) The moral issue of using up finite resources e.g. energy consumption in relation to population.

**Period 5 and 6**
*Sources:* Monkhouse and Wilkinson,
*Maps and Diagrams –* Methuen

(a) Exercise on mapping population distribution at various scales using dots, choropleths, isopleths and proportional divided circles.
(b) Analysis of what each method and each scale reveals.

**Period 7**
*Source: City of Birmingham Structure Plan –* City of Birmingham Planning Dept.

Examination of a case study of population distribution in an urban area by socio-economic group.
Discussion nature of classification and their limitations.

**Period 8**
*Source:* (b) Bradford and Kent *Human Geography*, p.173, O.U.P.

(a) From students experience attempt a typology of migrations; (i) spatially, (ii) over time.
(b) Exercise on mapping population flows.

**Period 9**
*Sources:* (a) *Geographical Magazine* Oct. 1968 — 'Calcutta a city in despair'.

Examination of the case of:
(a) Calcutta and its surrounding region to note causes and effect of rural to urban migration.

(b) Bradford and Kent
*Human Geography*,
O.U.P.
**Period 10**
*Source:* (i) Demko,
*Population
Geography*,
McGraw Hill
(ii) Zelinsky, *A
Prologue to Popu-
lation Geography*,
Prentice Hall

(b) Venezuela, to show causes of population movement in an oil-rich, developing
country.

Student research into causes of population
migration historically — Output is an essay
on 'The economic and social influences on
migrations of peoples'.

Discussion on the social consequences of
migrations e.g. Birmingham, London, New
York.

*EVALUATION*
(a) Formative or concurrent evaluation by the teacher based on
the output of course work by students.
(b) Special exercises in end of year test.
(c) Student evaluation through brief open ended questionnaire.

**Summary and conclusion**
Planning a sixth-form course in geography is, if anything, more
complex than planning a lower school course on account of the
likely variations not just in the students likely to follow an 'A' level
type or a non 'A' level type of course, but also because of the
possible variations which may occur if the 'N' and 'F' level system
is introduced. As indicated, these variations involve deciding on
the choices to be given to students and the depth to which a topic
will be treated. However, given the acceptance of broad general
aims, and the choice of a particular paradigm of geography, it is
possible to outline the content of such a course, and to devise
modules of work. Within these modules are contained the objectives
to be achieved and some indication of the way they may be achieved.
The teacher will no doubt use a more detailed plan for each unit
of work within the module. The whole 16–19 geography curriculum
is under review by the Geography 16–19 Schools Council Project,
and ideas on curriculum development at that level will no doubt
evolve rapidly in the next few years.

## CHAPTER SEVEN

# Aids for and Constraints on Curriculum Planning

## Introduction

The teacher may justifiably feel somewhat overwhelmed by the task of curriculum planning for geography. Fortunately he can now rely on help from several sources. First there are those agencies set up in the nineteen-sixties, whose main function is to foster curriculum development in one form or another. These may be national bodies, like the Nuffield Foundation and the Schools Council, or more limited local bodies like teachers' curriculum study groups set up partly by local education authorities and partly by subject associations, like the West Midlands Geography Teachers' Study Group. Secondly, there are bodies whose main purpose is to provide a wide variety of resources which teachers may use in the process of developing their curricula, for example, many publishers now also produce materials, other than books, for school use.

The purpose of this chapter is to outline the nature of the aids available and to attempt to evaluate these in terms of the teacher's curriculum planning task. Another but secondary purpose will be to look at the constraints on curriculum planning set by such institutions as examinations and by the attitudes of teachers, parents and society at large.

## National curriculum development agencies

Although one could argue that such associations as the Geographical Association, the Scottish Association of Geography Teachers and the Association of Geography Teachers of Ireland are curriculum development agencies, their functions are much wider and pre-date the present conception of curriculum development. The term 'curriculum development' is itself of relatively recent origin and implies an attempt to improve the content, pedagogical procedures and evaluation of the curriculum. I realise that the word 'improve' begs all sorts of questions, but at the common-sense level, it implies making learning more effective, changing the content so that this corresponds, in the case of geography, to what contemporary research workers would recognise as part of the discipline within which they are working, and being clear about worthwhile aims and objectives. Agencies set up especially to promote curriculum development in this sense are a relatively recent phenomenon. In England and Wales, the Schools Council for the Curriculum and Examinations, founded in 1964, has probably been the most active in the field of geographical education. In relation to curriculum planning, its main contributions have been in the financing of four main curriculum development projects directly involving geography and three others in which geography has been marginally involved.

Let us first examine the contributions of the main geography projects. In chronological order they consisted of the 'Geography 14 to 18 Project' and 'Geography for the Young School Leaver Project' (GYSL) both started in 1970, the 'History, Geography and Social Science 8–13 Project' which started in 1971 and the 'Geography 16–19 Project' which began in 1976. Although all were concerned with courses of geography or geography interrelated to other subject areas, not all were concerned to the same extent with the problem of curriculum planning as it affects the teacher. The 'Geography for the Young School Leaver Project' (GYSL) produced a course which was published by Nelson's (1974/75) which not only gave teachers an outline of what might be taught, with suggested aims and objectives, but also provided an extensive supply of materials which teachers could use in putting the course into operation. There are also ample opportunities for the teacher to develop the course in directions suitable to the circumstances of the school. Nevertheless, the bulk of the planning is already done for the teacher, so that if courses on 'Man, land and leisure', on 'Cities and people' and on 'People, place and work' are appropriate for the school geography curriculum, then a teacher need only be concerned with the problem of adapting the course and its materials for the students in question, which itself may be no small problem, depending on the students. Teachers wishing to find out more about the GYSL project may either get in touch with the publishers, who also produce the twice-yearly *Teachers Talking about the GYSL Project*, or with one of the local co-ordinators whose addresses appear at the end of this chapter in Appendix A. The function of the local co-ordinators is to enable teachers to help one another in the use of the GYSL project's ideas and materials. If Schools Council Projects are to be judged by the number of teachers taking them up for use in their own schools, then this project has been among the most successful. Although, originally designed for adolescents who were expected to leave school at the earliest opportunity, it became clear that the ideas and materials of the project had more general validity. Thus, at the time of writing (1978) it is possible to take both a CSE and an 'O' level examination based on the project. The CSE examination in London (Metropolitan Regional Examination Board) is a Mode II examination (school based syllabus; externally set and marked paper) but it may also be taken through other CSE boards (see B.E.E. 49, May 1975 and Appendix B). The GCE examination is set by the Welsh Joint Education Committee and the Southern University Joint Board on behalf of other examining Boards. (*Teachers Talking* Vol.3 1976). Thus one can argue that the GYSL project ideas and materials are useful to all geography teachers or teachers of social studies irrespective of the kind of school taught in or of the characteristics of the students. Its use in one school is described by Alan Wheatly (1976).

The 'Geography 14–18 Project' (Geography 14–18) worked on a somewhat different principle from the GYSL project, believing fundamentally that no curriculum development would take place unless teachers became curriculum developers themselves. Consequently, its energies were devoted to engendering change in a limited number of schools, using the project team as change agents. It was very much concerned with curriculum planning at the school level. The project's ideas and strategies are explained in two main publications, *A new professionalism for a changing geography* (Hickman, G *et al* 1973) and *Geography 14–18: a handbook for school-based curriculum development* (Tolley, H. and Reynolds, J. B. 1977). From a teacher's point of view the latter publication is the more immediately useful since it contains not only suggestions about curriculum planning and management (Chapters 2 and 3) but examples of how individual teaching units may be developed, managed and assessed, based on the work of individual schools like Forest Hill School in S.E. London and Withywood School in Bristol. Further the 'Geography 14–18

Project' have published separately teaching units on 'Industry', 'Transport Networks', 'Population' and 'Urban Geography' (Schools Council 1978) which teachers may use both directly and as examples for developing their own teaching units.

One of the major achievements of the 'Geography 14–18 Project' was that of setting up a new G.C.E. 'O' level examination in geography. This followed from its model of the curriculum process, in which the project team saw G.C.E. examinations as an essential element in the system, and consequently argued that no curriculum change could take place if the examination was not changed. The Schools Council Geography 14–18 Project G.C.E. Ordinary Level Examination is administered on behalf of G.C.E. boards by the University of Cambridge Local Examinations Syndicate. This means that teachers wishing to use that examination must get in touch with the Cambridge Board irrespective of the examination board which they use at present. The distinctive features of the Geography 14–18 'O' level examination are that: 50% of the total marks are based on a common core curriculum, examined by an external examination paper; 30% of the marks are based on course work and 20% of the marks are based on an individual study. Both the course work and individual study are internally marked but externally moderated. The advantages of such a scheme are that teachers are less constrained by the external examination and may develop courses to suit their local circumstances and their students' apparent needs. The core syllabus is designed to cover ideas of general validity in geography in line with current trends in research at a higher level in education. Broadly the core curriculum's objectives are to promote an understanding of:

  (a)  the geographical character of the school's local area and of the British Isles as a whole,

  (b)  significant contrasts and similarities between the British Isles and other developed areas and developing areas,

  (c)  the workings of physical and economic systems at a world scale,

  (d)  the processes involved in landscape and other spatial patterns and how those engender change,

  (e)  environmental inter-relationships seen as systems involving cumulative and multiple causal relationships,

  (f)  the role of decision making in the context of people's values and perceptions,

(g) the importance of the scale at which spatial patterns are considered,

(h) how ideas, models and maps simplify complex reality.

The course work can be designed to study areas of the curriculum in greater depth and the assessment may concentrate on those aspects of study not easily assessed by a written examination, for example, the initiative and persistence shown by the candidate in following through a particular topic or problem. Examples and guidelines for developing course work and individual studies are contained in appendices of the handbook referred to above. It should be stated at the outset that though teachers may find the preparation of candidates for the Geography 14−18 'O'-level examination very rewarding, it inevitably involves a considerable increase in the teacher's work load in the initial stages. Nevertheless, teachers wishing to take up the challenge will be able to obtain help from local groups of teachers or consortia who want to help one another and diffuse ideas. The L.E.A. organiser may have information on these. Lastly, it ought to be made clear that although the Geography 14−18 Project originally intended to consider geography for the more able students from 14 to 18 years-of-age, it became clear, as in the case of the GYSL project, that its ideas were more generally applicable. It was unable, because of lack of time, to develop these ideas beyond the 16 year-old level. A teacher's view of the project has been presented by Tony Gelsthorpe (1976).

As there was a need to carry out curriculum development in geography at the 16−19 year-old level, the Schools Council launched a new project in October 1976 whose purpose was precisely to develop curricula in geography for students of *all* abilities in that age group. The four-person project team based on the University of London Institute of Education, is at the time of writing (January 1978) not yet half-way through its initial three-year life-span. It has recently had its life extended by another three years. In that brief time it has sent out and analysed a pilot questionnaire to obtain clues as to the perceived needs of students and teachers as well as to find out what the current situation and practices were in schools and tertiary colleges. It has also considered the contribution that geography can make to the 16−19 curriculum and outlined the broad aims of the subject at that level. It has considered the kinds of conceptual frameworks or paradigms available to geography teachers and decided to advocate the use of a single man-environment framework for curriculum planning at the 16–19 level. It has also produced a curriculum teaching unit (Hurricanes) as an exemplar. Lastly, the team has negotiated with the University of London School Examinations Board for the development of an experimental 'A' level examination in geography based on the project's work. If all goes well the first candidates could sit the new examination in June 1981 (Naish 1976, 1978).

In the 'field' the project team is working with ten pilot groups with one to three pilot schools or colleges within each group. Each group has a local co-ordinator and a local authority representative. The pilot groups are responsible for implementing and experimenting with the project's ideas and suggestions. Since the project's policy is one of joint initiatives: by the project team at the centre and by the pilot schools at the periphery, the pilot schools have an important role in the process of curriculum change and innovation. There are also associate schools linked to the project and the pilot schools. These perform similar functions to those of the pilot schools, but because of the team's small size, receive less direct stimulation from the project team. The location of the local education authorities cooperating with the Geography 16–19 Project is shown in the map on Figure 7.1. Papers which summarize the project's approach and work so far are the *Project News, Broad Aims for Geography in the 16–19 Age Group* and *A Framework for the Geography Curriculum 16–19,* published by project.

At the lower school level, the curriculum development project which has most to offer is the 'History, Geography and Social Science Project 8–13', which was concerned with the middle-school age range. The project's most substantial publication is entitled *Curriculum Planning in History, Geography and Social Science* (Blyth *et al* 1976) and contains a section on the 'contribution of geography' to the 8–13 curriculum, as well as suggested guide lines for curriculum planning involving the consideration of aims and objectives, of sequencing and evaluation. A special feature of the project which may be of considerable value to those planning curricula in the lower secondary school is the emphasis on the interrelatedness of various subjects. This, the project attempted to do through the use of what they called the 'key concepts' of 'communication', 'power', 'values and beliefs', 'conflict and consensus', 'similarity and difference', 'continuity and change', and 'causality'. Teachers may also find useful booklets entitled 'Themes in outline', 'Games and simulation in the classroom', 'Teaching for CONCEPTS', 'Evaluation, assess-

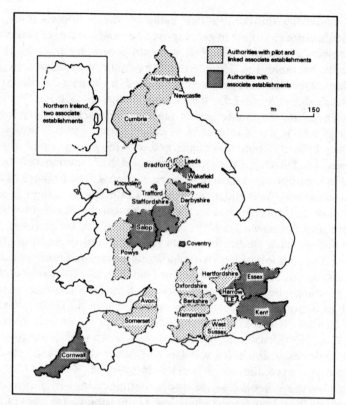

FIGURE 7.1. Geography 16–19 Project. Distribution of LEAs having formal school and college links with the project.

ment and record keeping in history, geography and social science', 'Teaching for empathy' 'Teaching critical thinking skills', 'Using Social Statistics' and 'Using sources and resources'. These are all suggestions for curriculum planning and teaching strategies. The project has also produced some teaching units which may be used in the classroom geography such as 'Rivers in flood', 'People on the move; a study of migration', 'Villages and towns: a study of changing communities', 'Points, patterns and movement: detective work in geography', 'People and progress: a study of cultures at risk' and 'The geography of hunger'. All these may be obtained from Collins – E.S.L. acting on behalf of the Schools Council. The working of the project in a school may be read in Gordon Elliott's article (1976) in *Developments in Geography*.

In reviewing the contribution made by the Schools Council to curriculum development in geography, one must not forget that made by projects whose main interests were not geography as such. There were for example, the 'Humanities Curriculum Project' whose curriculum planning strategies are exemplified in Chapter 2 in the Stenhouse model (Figure 2.5), the 'Keele Integrated Studies Project' which has published materials through the Oxford University Press, some of which are of relevance to geographers, and the 'Resource Centres Project' which was concerned with the storage and retrieval systems used in school resource centres which are increasingly being used in the implementation of modern curricula. The findings of this last project may be found in the Schools Council's Working Paper 43 (1972) or in Norman Beswick's (the Research officer involved) *Organising Resources* (1975). The latter book is much fuller and contains six case studies of school resource centres and how they work. The schools were two senior high schools (John Smeaton School, Leeds and Heywood Senior High School, Lancashire), two 11-18 comprehensive schools (Codsall School, Staffordshire, and Nailsea School, Somerset), one grammar school (Fakenham Grammar School, Norfolk) and one middle school (Greneway School, Royston, Hertfordshire). The case studies give a useful indication of how each resource centre was laid out, what storage and retrieval system was used and how it worked in practice.

Outside the Schools Council (and sometimes within it) the group of Her Majesty's Inspectors who have responsibility for geography, help by issuing statements of curriculum aims and objectives and by making suggestions for content. One such publication is *The teaching of ideas in geography. Some suggestions for the middle and secondary years of education* (H.M.S.O. 1978). This is a most useful source of ideas for the teacher who is wondering what to include or leave out in the geography curriculum. It represents the product of much thought and discussion as well as the distillation of years of experience on the part of those involved in the drafting. The first part consists of a brief but useful discussion of the nature of concepts and generalizations, of models and systems, of decision making and perception, of skills and attitudes and lastly of the idea of progression in the learning of geography. The second part is essentially a classified list of generalizations which might form the basis of geography courses. For example the first generalization under the heading of 'Landforms' is 'The earth's crust is composed of a number of mobile plates and the formation and distribution of oceans, continents, major relief features, volcanic activity and earthquakes, reflect the interaction between them'. Teaching units on plate tectonics could be designed to achieve an understanding by students of that generalization. The third part of the booklet consists of suggestions on the use of these generalizations in the classroom context.

## Local curriculum development agencies

It is much more difficult to write with the same assurance about local agencies as about the Schools Council. In the first place less publicity is attached to these and there are many variations in the functions of these local agencies. What in fact are they?

In most cases they are simply groups of teachers who have got together to discuss and attempt to solve a particular problem, or who have an abiding interest in a particular aspect of geography, such as geography as a means to environmental education.

Let us take the case of London and in particular the ILEA (Inner London Education Authority). This will enable us to examine the relationship between a national curriculum development project (GYSL) and local teacher initiative. The use of the GYSL project materials is fairly widespread in London schools, partly because the project was first developed in the London area and the process of diffusion naturally affected London first of all. It is also true that the ILEA advisory service (the inspectors) has always taken a keen interest in the project and that finance has been available to buy the project's kits of materials. Thus, teachers using the project and others interested in it have met regularly at four different Teachers' Centres in London. Their activities, encouraged by the ILEA advisory teachers, have led to the production of supplementary materials suitable to illustrate ideas based on London examples and to the ILEA television service producing programmes based on the project. (Tumman 1977).

Another example is that of the West Midlands Geography Teachers' Groups. This is a group of teachers which has met regularly with a view to undertaking curriculum development and dealing with certain problems in geographical education. Based partly on the Department of Education at the University of Birmingham, the group has become particularly active in the field of sixth-form geography. In 1974 the groups produced, helped by a Schools Council grant, an outline for a new 'A' level curriculum in geography (West Midlands Geography Teachers Study Group 1974). In 1976 a nucleus of the group was asked by the Schools Council's 18+ steering groups to produce a suggested curriculum document outlining the aims, objectives, content and method of evaluation for modular geography course, based on the Schools Council's proposals for a five-subject curriculum (the 'N' & 'F' proposals) for the 16–19 age groups. This the group did and its recommendations were published. (Schools Council 1977 a b).

Local Education Authorities may also undertake vigorous activities in curriculum development not necessarily based on a National Curriculum Development project. For example the Hertfordshire L.E.A, in conjunction with a local adviser and interested teachers, worked for several years on an 'Environmental Studies' curriculum for 'A' level students, which was eventually accepted by the University of London Examinations Board (University of London 1978) and by the Schools Council (which has a statutory duty to vet all 'A' level examinations). Similarly, the corporation of Glasgow Education Department has produced many schemes of work and curricula suitable for geography and modern studies, as has the Scottish Centre for Social Subjects.

In general, most informal groups are based on local teachers' centres and an enquiry from the advisory teacher in charge (or Warden) will indicate whether a geography group is meeting regularly or not. The great advantage of such centres is the interchange of ideas which goes on, thereby helping to break down the traditional isolation of the teacher. Further, such teachers' centres have audio-visual and reprographic facilities which enable the rapid production of teaching materials in a way sometimes not possible in individual schools. A good example is the Manchester Geography Teachers' Centre located in the Manchester Polytechnic. Sometimes such centres exist in colleges of education and in University Departments of Education. For example, the University of London Institute of Education has such a centre called the University Centre for Teachers which is a resource centre as well as a centre for courses and conferences. Thus teacher-training institutions often provide useful help with curriculum problems. Branches of the Geographical Association may also function in a similar way as agencies for the diffusion and development of new curricula as well as for more traditional purposes. Workshop sessions at such meetings involve teachers in the production of teaching schemes and teaching units.

## Commercial and non-commercial aids

The vast amount of published material now available makes the task of choosing a difficult one. Commercial publishers are clearly more concerned with providing teachers with resources for classroom use than in the task of curriculum planning itself, though the availability of particular resources will be one of the factors involved in curriculum planning. While some teachers may base their courses on a particular textbook or textbook series, it is seldom possible to do this satisfactorily because of the influence on curriculum of local conditions and examinations. Consequently the teacher must choose among the commercially published resources those which appear to best suit his purpose within the limitations imposed by finance. To help the teacher in this task, the University of Sussex Centre for Educational Technology has produced a 'Scheme for the Analysis of Curriculum Materials'.

Broadly the suggestion is that the teacher might go about the evaluation of curriculum materials in a systematic way, so that the same criteria would be consistently applied to all materials. The scheme as presented in Appendix C at the end of this chapter, is divided into four parts; each part consisting essentially of questions to bring out the nature and utility of the materials in the educational process. Part I asks questions about the published nature of the materials as given by the author and publisher, including the author's credentials, avowed objectives and the target population characteristics. Part II is a more detailed analysis of the materials with a view to finding out the precise nature of the contents; language used, illustrations, the student exercises, the detailed content areas covered. Part III is concerned to establish how the materials might be used, with what curriculum, with what other teaching aids, with which teaching strategies and so on. Part IV suggests an evaluation of the aims, strategy, and suitability of the materials in the particular context envisaged. Part V not reproduced in detail in Appendix C, is the stage at which a rationale for a decision is given in terms of the constraints on the curriculum and school in question, the possible use and the strategies required to put the materials into operation. The teacher must decide whether he uses the whole scheme or makes a summary judgment based on those questions which are most relevant to his case. An elaborate attempt at evaluating a curriculum based on two textbooks may be found in Lidstone (1977.) One useful technique in selecting books is to apply the Flesch Readability Score, which indicates broadly the reading age for which the text is suitable. (See Appendix D).

The kinds of resources available range from textbook series, individual texts, special publications by non-commercial charities of one sort or another like the Association of Agriculture and the Centre for World Development Education, audio-tapes, like the Sussex tapes, video tapes of television programmes, filmstrips and illustrated pamphlets to be used with recorded BBC radio programmes (Radio vision), films, work cards, short texts based on themes like 'Harrap's Reformed Geography Series' and at a lower level the 'Macdonald Colour Geography', overhead projector transparencies, slides and so on. One method of checking on what is available and what is new is to attend the publishers' exhibition at the Annual Conference of the Geographical Association. Here the teacher may stroll at leisure through the exhibition and pick up catalogues and other sources of information. Another, but less up-to-date method is to use a handbook like the *Handbook for Geography Teachers* published for the University of London Institute of Education (Long 1974). The University of London Institute of Education also houses the National Textbook Library which may be consulted by teachers. Similarly, the Geographical Association has a large library of textbooks from which members may borrow.

### Constraints on curriculum planning

The various teaching materials available are not only aids to curriculum implementation, they may well result in curriculum innovation, since teachers may first come across a worthwhile idea in a textbook, or a film or other aid. It is therefore worthwhile looking on the positive side first and attempting to find ways of making a particular geography course more interesting, not to say exciting, always granted that this is something worth learning. Value judgments are an inevitable part of any teacher's job. But it would be unrealistic not to accept that there is a considerable number of constraints on curriculum planning which the teacher must take into account and attempt to work with if they cannot be overcome.

I am not concerned here with the more immediate 'tactical' constraints imposed by, for example, a particular timetable structure, but by the broader, more long-term constraints imposed by societal attitudes (including student and teacher attitudes) and those imposed by institutions such as examination boards.

Let me begin by examining attitudes. This is not an easy task as attitudes are notoriously difficult to assess accurately and objectively; indeed the task may be almost impossible, since the investigator has himself a bundle of subjective attitudes which he cannot discard. I can only write about the 'common sense' view of attitudes, that is of attitudes which are manifest in the way people talk and behave, bearing in mind that a verbally expressed attitude may be different from an attitude expressed through behaviour in the same person. There is little evidence that society at large has any definite attitude about geography and the geography curriculum. Whereas it is possible to glean information about the views of employers and parents about the literacy and numeracy aspect of the curriculum, seldom do parents and employers, as a whole, say anything about geography. Indeed when 'lay' individuals do speak out, it is to reveal a rather outmoded view of geography, in which factual information is the main component. This is largely because many parents and employers tend to have an instrumental view of education and therefore of geographical education, as a kind of vocational training. The main problem, therefore, is to modernize the image of geography among the public at large. In general, the attitude of parents and employers appears to be either neutral or mildly favourable but misguidedly so. It is thought by some employers that geography teachers have not done their job, if their newest recruit does not know some place names significant to the organizations in question. The only possible constraint which might be thought to emanate from such a source, might be the perceived need by the curriculum planner to include in the contextual examples used, those areas which are economically significant to the United Kingdom, for example more emphasis might be given to the European Economic Community than to Africa.

The attitudes of teachers, are probably much more significant, since how they perceive a proposed curriculum change is crucial in determining whether it will be implemented or not. There is in most of us an unacknowledged (sometimes it is acknowledged) desire to keep things as they are. This is manifest in groups and institutions, in what Donald Schon (1971) has called 'dynamic conservatism', a kind of will to maintain the status quo, which may be transformed into action for that purpose. This is almost inevitable, since change presents us with a challenge and can be perceived as a threat. It is easier and less worrying to carry on doing what we have learned to do well than to attempt something new, something of which we are unsure, where our success is not guaranteed. The older we are the less we are inclined to expose our ignorance or our lack of skill. I remember feeling somewhat mortified when I found myself on a data processing course with people half my age who often seemed to be making more rapid progress than I was! Similarly, within the confines of my own department I have to fight against the tendency to maintain a course in its present form when suggestions are made to alter it. Teachers within school geography departments are subject to the same kinds of conservative tendencies, but how much they succumb to them depends on a number of factors, such as the number of teachers in the department, the average age and the frequency of contact with colleagues in other schools. Change does not necessarily mean change for the better and any proposed change needs to be examined in the light of criteria for worthwhileness. But teachers need to maintain an open mind about curriculum development and beware of discouraging young colleagues who are eager to introduce an innovation. By examining the innovation carefully and modifying it to suit the school situation, the older teacher can make his wisdom gathered over the years, serve profitably the cause of curriculum improvement. Further, if curriculum innovations are brought in gradually in a piecemeal fashion, they are much more likely to prove acceptable and in practice easier to assimilate within a course than if an attempt is made to revolutionize the school course 'at a stroke'.

Students and pupils can be as conservative as their teachers. Much depends on what experiences they have had and therefore also on their age. The younger the students, the less experience of the subject they have, the less likely they are to have preconceived notions of what geography is and ought to be. This is partly why innovations in curricula are often easier to introduce in primary and lower secondary age groups than in the higher age groups. Students of 15 to 16 years will argue when presented with an exercise on networks, that this work is not geography, because they have a preconceived idea of geography as a description of countries or regions. I do not want to overstress the conservatism of students, for in practice resistance to particular curricula is more likely for reasons that have little to do with the conservatism of students, but more to the socio-cultural context within which the students are working.

Much more significant is the influence of various institutions linked to the school system, of which probably the most important are the examination boards. I would like to make clear that what follows is not an attack on these boards but an analysis of the kind of relationships which made conservatism almost inevitable. Examination boards have constitutions which regulate the way each board works. Thus there may be a council which is the policy making body, an advisory or subject panel for each subject examined, chief examiners for each subject and a panel of assistant examiners. Members of the policy and advisory committees tend to be the more senior members of the teaching profession (Bruce 1969) and though with valuable experience to offer, they may not always take kindly to new ideas. Further, chief examiners who may be secondary school teachers and/or teachers in higher education, are also likely to be persons who have served long apprenticeships as assistant examiners. It is they who set the questions and devise the marking schemes. The assistant examiners are usually chosen from among teachers with several years of experience. Their role is essentially a technical one of assessing candidates in the light of the marking scheme devised by the chief examiner. In my own personal experience, though the marking scheme is discussed with the chief examiner at an examiners' meeting after the examination has been sat, there is little encouragement to assistants to upset the apple cart. Similarly, questions set by the chief examiners are vetted by a moderator, who is a kind of father figure who checks that the questions are in accordance with the published syllabus and that they are unlikely to be unfair to candidates. This makes the moderator's job essentially a conservative one, since all innovatory questions are likely to appear unfair to some candidates. Thus, though the examination board may welcome curriculum innovation, its very workings make such innovation difficult. In the case of geography, it required a very concerted campaign and many meetings between teachers and the boards' representatives before change occurred as a result of the conceptual revolution of the 1960s. The Oxford and Cambridge Board was the first to change its syllabuses in geography at 'A' level in the late 1960s; subsequently, other examination boards followed suit, though not in identical ways. The problem is that though the present membership of the advisory panels may be favourable to the recent changes, it follows that these may become the conservative establishment of tomorrow. The same is true of the C.S.E. boards which were created from 1965 onwards. Many of the members of the subject panels appointed in the 1960s were enthusiastic for changes in examination procedures and subject content. But these could now be well satisfied with what was then achieved and resist further change.

The problem is how to ensure that the constraints imposed upon curriculum planning by the existence of examination boards are not too restrictive. One way is to make the boards themselves more amenable to change than they have apparently been in the past. This might be achieved in two ways. First, by making curriculum revision a compulsory exercise every 10 years. I put it at no shorter interval simply because I am aware of the various consultation processes necessary to admit a change in the curriculum. This, in my view, would force the issue and both new ideas could be inserted and 'deadwood' content pruned out. Secondly, the membership of advisory panels should also change at regular intervals, so that members were compulsorily retired after five years' service. New members could be obtained from the teacher unions but more importantly, from younger active teacher members of the relevant geographical bodies like the Geographical Association and the Institute of British Geographers as well as the Royal Geographical Society.

Another way of limiting the restrictive effects of boards is for the school to operate on a Mode 3 in C.S.E. and/or in G.C.E. The energy required to do this is considerable and I do not underestimate the difficulties created for schools who wish to operate on a school-based syllabus and on school-examined, externally moderated examinations. For G.C.E. examinations, a true Mode 3 system is not as yet generally available, though the Geography 14 – 18 project examination approximates to this.

**Summary and conclusions**

In the 1950s and early 1960s, the teacher, intent on curriculum development and replanning his syllabus, was in a relatively lonely situation. He might have obtained help from his local inspector or advisor; he might have gone on a D.E.S. course, or to his local Institute of Education; but apart from what he could glean in the few books on geographical education, he would have been thrown back on his own ingenuity and that of his colleagues. The pressure of day to day teaching and extra-curricula activity meant that the time available for rethinking curricula was limited. Now things have changed, largely due to the influence of the major national curriculum development projects. Teachers are not only able to use courses devised by those having more time to think out radical changes in content and teaching strategies, but in many small different but significant ways, their practice has been affected by the materials made available. Thus curriculum planning in geography within a school is a process which, in spite of the undoubted constraints which exist (finance, examination), is facilitated by the various agencies and resources which are now available. Nevertheless, the teacher is still the king pin of the whole operation. No curriculum materials, no matter how well devised, will automatically ensure that students and pupils will learn and enjoy learning. The art of curriculum planning whether at the general level or at the instructional level requires time and energy. I believe that teachers will only really be able to undertake such tasks professionally when they are given less face-to-face teaching to do and more planning and preparation time.

# Appendix A to Chapter Seven

*Publishers of the Geography for the Young School Leaver Project:*
The Educational Sales Department, Thomas Nelson and Sons Ltd., Lincoln Way, Windmill Road, Sunbury on Thames, Middlesex TW16 7HP. Telephone Sunbury 85681.

*Regional Co-ordinators for the GYSL Project*

**Greater London/Home Counties**
Lesley Turnman, Advisory Teacher for Geography, Teachers' Centre Avery Hill College, Avery Hill Road, London SE9 2PQ.

**Home Counties West (Surrey, Berkshire, Hampshire, Buckinghamshire)**
Mary Allwood, Senior Lecturer in Geography, Berkshire College of Education, Bulmershe Court, Woodlands Avenue, Earley, Reading RG6 1HY.

**South-West England**
John Hancock, Head of Geography, St Paul's College of Education, Cheltenham, Gloucestershire, GL50 4AZ.

**Wales**
Muriel John, Senior Lecturer in Geography, City of Cardiff College of Education, Cyncoed, Cardiff, CF2 6XD.

**West Midlands**
Bob Prosser, Head of Geography, St Peter's College of Education, Saltley, Birmingham, B8 3TE.

**East Anglia**
Bob Arthur, Senior Lecturer in Geography, Homerton College, Cambridge, CB2 2PH.

**South Yorkshire**
Trevor Higginbottom, City of Sheffield Education Dept. P.O. Box 67, Leopold Street, Sheffield, S1 1RJ.

**Mid-West**
(Cheshire, Liverpool, Wirral, Sefton, Shropshire, Staffordshire, St Helens, Derbyshire),
John Tresadern, Lecturer in Geography, Matlock College of Education, Derbyshire.

**North-West England**
Nigel Proctor, Senior Lecturer in Geography, Didsbury College of Education, Wilmslow Road, Manchester, M20 8RR.

**North-East England**
Dick Race, Director, Regional Curriculum Development Unit, Northumberland College of Education, Ponteland, Newcastle-upon-Tyne, NE20 0AB.

**Northern Ireland**
Eric Woods, Adviser for Environmental Studies, South Eastern Education and Library Board, 18 Windsor Avenue, Belfast BT9 6EF.

**Scotland**
Douglas McCreath, Lecturer in Education, Notre Dame College of Education, Bearsden, Glasgow G61 4QA.

# Appendix B to Chapter Seven

*Extracts* from the Wilsthorpe School Syllabus prepared by the GYSL Project's Derbyshire Curriculum Group – Co-ordinator John Tresadern, Matlock College of Education. (This scheme has now been modified, but the general principles are similar.)

## INTRODUCTION

The 'Geography for the Young School Leaver' Project on which this syllabus is based has been produced with strong reference to changes taking place in Geography and in Education. The changes necessitate the constant clarification and up-dating of teaching objectives and procedures. In the long term, the aim of the Project is not only to develop innovatory styles of learning and teaching, but to enable teachers to plan and structure their own curricula more effectively. It is important to be aware of the way such developments are reflected in the Project to appreciate the key structures of this syllabus.

1. Developments in Curriculum Planning have highlighted the importance of the identification of objectives. This Project identifies three types of objectives:
    a) Key Ideas – often important concepts, serving as focal points for the selection of content.
    b) Skills – intellectual and social.
    c) Values and attitudes.

2. Developments in Geography have been associated with the growth from a purely descriptive discipline to one that seeks to be explanatory. The search for explanation is producing a body of spatial theory which relates to the common elements in spatial distributions. This emphasis on theory, with its generalisations and models on one hand, and its potential for prediction on the other, is in line with developments in other physical and social sciences. The main implications for geography in schools is that while there must be full use of case-study and direct observation in the field, the ultimate aim should be the understanding of ideas – ideas relating to location, pattern and process. This applies to pupils of all ages and abilities. Such key ideas are clearly identified in this Project and form its working base.

3. Developments in Styles of Learning have emphasised the importance of child-active and child-centred learning situations. This

syllabus is based on a Project that offers a wide range of resources. These are intended to be used flexibly by the teacher to enable him to design learning experiences which will lead to the achievement of the stated objectives. Essentially, however, by seeking answers to problems it is intended that individual thinking should be encouraged replacing memorisation as a dominant classroom activity.

4. Developments in thinking on Evaluation demand that evaluation should be to assess whether or not the objectives of any teaching programme have been achieved; and not merely used as a device for grading and ranking pupils. The evaluation items of this syllabus are all designed to relate to clearly specified objectives.

## AIMS AND OBJECTIVES

*SYLLABUS AIMS:*
1. That education should be concerned with all aspects of pupil development — knowledge, skills and attitudes.
2. That the learning process must encourage involvement and active participation, therefore the content of the course must be relevant to the lives of the pupils, both in terms of topics studied and methods of study, now and in the future.
3. That the particular concepts and skills involved in geography can play an important part in improving young people's understanding of their environment at local, national and world scales.

*SYLLABUS OBJECTIVES:*
1. That pupils should acquire geographical concepts and ideas related to the contemporary themes of 'Leisure', 'Urbanisation', and 'Work.'
2. To promote skills related to the use of maps, photographs, statistics and textual data.
3. To involve the pupils in the area of attitudes and values so they may examine opinions with consideration, tolerance and understanding.
4. That pupils should learn at several levels so as:
   a) to be able to store information and recall it later.
   b) to understanding knowledge involved in the studies.
   c) to be able to apply knowledge and experience gained to new problems.
   d) to be able to make their own reasoned judgments and evaluations of problems/issues.

## SYLLABUS CONTENT

Details of the topics and objectives of each theme in the Project and Syllabus are presented:
1. Key Idea Objectives.
2. Skill Objectives.
3. Attitudes and Value Objectives.
4. Topics – indicating local, national and world cover.

These Tables set out a framework basis of the syllabus. In an 'ideas based' syllabus such as this, the content must be viewed as a means to an end and not an end in itself. With more than one school using the syllabus, actual case studies selected will vary – particularly at the local scale. Furthermore it is intended that additional materials will be developed to offer alternatives to present resources and to extend the range of ideas.

### 1   KEY IDEA OBJECTIVES
#### THEME: PEOPLE, PLACE AND WORK

| UNIT/PART | SUMMARY OF KEY IDEAS |
|---|---|
| **UNIT 1** | **WHY WORK?** |
| **Part 1 Work for what?** | While most people regard work primarily in terms of earning a living; many need to feel that their work is significant and contributing in some way to society. |
| **Part 2 People in and out of work** | In the last decade there have been marked changes in the structure of employment. Unemployment has resulted where there has been a decline in the demand for labour. |
| **Part 3 Work and leisure** | A shorter working day/week, forecast for the future, will have implications for the use of non-work time. |
| **UNIT 2** | **PATTERNS OF WORK** |
| **Part 1 Places and Work** | Some types of work have to be located at sites determined by physical conditions. Where choice of site is available the most profitable is usually chosen, i.e. where costs of raw materials, fuel and power, labour, transport, etc. are minimised, and where there exists a large demand for the product or service. Many work units are part of larger organisations and depend on decisions made elsewhere. There is a tendency for the size of work units to increase to benefit from the advantages of large-scale production. |

| UNIT/PART | SUMMARY OF KEY IDEAS |
| --- | --- |
| **Part 2 Journey to Work** | Some people live near their place of work, others a long way away. Accessibility and availability of transport influence the distance workers travel and thus affect their choice of work locations. |
| **Part 3 Occupational structures — city, region and state** | Employment structures of towns and regions have many common elements but variations due to specialisation can be identified. |

Another excerpt from the syllabus for People, Place and Work:

| UNIT/PART | SUMMARY OF KEY IDEAS |
| --- | --- |
| **Part 3 Concentration within the city** | Metropolitan cities and large urban centres are the main reception areas for immigrants. Certain areas of cities, often inner zones, attract new immigrant groups. There is a tendency for concentration in these areas because of availability of accommodation, the wish of people of similar background to be together or because of external pressures. |
| **Part 4 Change within the city** | There is often centrifugal movement of city population as the demand for better housing and space standards is met by new house construction on the edge of the city. The movement may be spontaneous or planned. A neighbourhood may pass through a cycle of change. There is residential succession as the original population is displaced — or replaced by another. |
| **Part 5 Moving out of cities** | It is sometimes necessary for people to move out of cities, particularly from the inner areas. Contributing factors include the inadequacy of housing, the general environment and the changing pattern of work opportunities. Dispersion has meant that some cities have experienced a recent decline in population. The areas to which people go vary from new villages and towns to overspill additions to existing communities. |

| UNIT/PART | SUMMARY OF KEY IDEAS |
|---|---|
| **UNIT 5** | **PLANNING FOR CITIES** |
| **Part 1 Planning for the local area**<br>**Part 2 Planning for the region** | Planners have considerable influence over the quality of the urban environment.<br>There are various scales of planning — for example at the local and regional level.<br>When making their decisions planners have to decide on the relative emphases which need to be given to the promotion of social harmony, economic efficiency and the aesthetic aspects of the environment.<br>Planners are almost always faced with cost constraints. |
| **Suggestions for community involvement** | Individuals or organisations often bring pressure to bear in order to influence planning decisions. |
| **UNIT 6** | **THE FUTURE IN BRITAIN** |
| **Part 1 Housing — what sort of provision?** | Changing life styles will lead to increasing demand on space in the environment. |
| **Part 2 Scarcity of land — true or false?** | If urban growth continues at its present rate, land shortage will be a crucial problem. |
| **Part 3 Transport — do we have a choice?** | As central areas become more congested, there may be restrictions on the type of transport permitted. |

## 2 SKILL OBJECTIVES

| | Man, Land and Leisure Units | | | | | Cities and People Units | | | | | | People, Place and Work Units | | | | | |
|---|---|---|---|---|---|---|---|---|---|---|---|---|---|---|---|---|---|
| | 1 | 2 | 3 | 4 | 5 | 1 | 2 | 3 | 4 | 5 | 6 | 1 | 2 | 3 | 4 | 5 | 6 |
| 1. Use an atlas | × | | | | | × | × | × | × | × | × | | × | × | × | × | × |
| 2. Read maps of different types | | × | × | × | × | × | × | × | × | × | × | | × | × | × | × | × |
| 3. Make a simple map transformation | | | × | × | | | | | | | | | × | | | | |
| 4. Correlate an air photograph with a map | | × | | × | | × | | | × | | | | × | | × | | |
| 5. Record and analyse weather and climatic data | | | × | × | | | | | | | | | × | | | | |
| 6. Make an annotated landscape sketch from a photograph | | | × | × | | | × | | | | | | × | | | × | |
| 7. Make field observations | × | | × | | | × | × | × | | | | | × | | | | |
| 8. Analyse an air photograph | | × | × | | | × | × | | × | | | × | × | × | × | × | × |
| 9. Interpret data | × | × | × | × | | × | × | × | | | | × | × | × | × | × | × |
| 10. Interpret visual information | × | × | × | × | × | × | × | × | | × | | × | × | × | × | × | |
| 11. Analyse graphs | × | × | × | × | | × | × | × | | | | × | × | × | × | | |
| 12. Represent statistics graphically | | × | × | × | | × | × | × | × | | | | × | × | × | | |
| 13. Compare information from different sources | × | × | × | × | | × | × | × | × | × | × | × | × | × | × | | |
| 14. Make analysis of printed and tape recorded information | × | × | × | × | × | × | | × | × | × | × | | × | × | × | | |
| 15. Formulate and test hypothesis | × | × | × | × | | × | × | × | × | × | × | | × | × | × | × | |
| 16. Engage in role play and discussion | × | × | × | × | | × | × | × | × | × | × | × | × | × | × | × | |
| 17. Creative expression — written, oral, drawn | × | × | × | | × | × | × | × | × | × | × | | × | × | | × | × |

# 3 ATTITUDES AND VALUE OBJECTIVES

## MAN, LAND AND LEISURE

| VALUES AND ATTITUDES — | U1 Pt.1 Use of leisure time | U1 Pt.2 Pattern of leisure activity | U1 Pt.3 Increasing amount of leisure time | U1 Pt.4 Leisure Pursuits in the Past | U2 Pt.1 Local Study – indoor and outdoor | U2 Pt.2 Inner City Study | U2 Pt.3 Open space in a conurbation | U2 Pt.4 Planned urban areas | U2 Pt.5 Future town shapes | U3 Pt.1 National Parks of England and Wales | U3 Pt.2 The Peak District N.P. | U4 Pt.1 Patterns of holidays | U4 Pt.2 British Seaside Holiday Resorts | U4 Pt.3 A holiday environment | U4 Pt.4 Holiday environments in W. Europe | U4 Pt.5 Holidays and the travel industry | U4 Pt.6 Seasonal nature of holidays | U4 Pt.7 Tourism as big business | U5 The future |
|---|---|---|---|---|---|---|---|---|---|---|---|---|---|---|---|---|---|---|---|
| 1. About the 'quality' of the environment. | ✓ | ✓ | ✓ | ✓ | ✓ | ✓ | | | | ✓ | ✓ | ✓ | ✓ | ✓ | ✓ | | | | |
| 2. About the 'quality of life' of individuals within particular environments. | | ✓ | ✓ | ✓ | | | | | | | | | | | | | | | ✓ |
| 3. About the apparent inequalities within society. | | | | | | | | | | | | ✓ | | | | | | | |
| 4. About the need to both accommodate and question change in the environment. | | | | | | | ✓ | | | ✓ | ✓ | | | | | | | | |
| 5. About the way in which change may affect the individual. | | | | | | | | | | | | | | ✓ | | | | | |
| 6. About the need to retain individual identity within large scale organisations and environments. | | | | | | | | ✓ | | | | | ✓ | ✓ | | | | ✓ | |
| 7. About the need to examine both sides of a viewpoint. | | | | | ✓ | | | | | | | | ✓ | | | | | | |
| 8. About the dilemmas involved in preserving individual freedom on the one hand and on the other the need for society to be restrictive for the benefit of the majority. | | | | | | | | ✓ | ✓ | | | | | | | | | | |
| 9. About the individual's responsibilities for action taken which will affect future generations. | | | | | | | | | | ✓ | | | | | | | | | |

Column groupings:

- **Unit 1 — Leisure Time:** Pt.1 Use of leisure time; Pt.2 Pattern of leisure activity; Pt.3 Increasing amount of leisure time; Pt.4 Leisure Pursuits in the Past
- **Unit 2 — Local Communities:** Pt.1 Local Study – indoor and outdoor; Pt.2 Inner City Study; Pt.3 Open space in a conurbation; Pt.4 Planned urban areas; Pt.5 Future town shapes
- **Unit 3 — National Parks:** Pt.1 National Parks of England and Wales; Pt.2 The Peak District N.P.
- **Unit 4 — Leisure and Tourism in Britain and Western Europe:** Pt.1 Patterns of holidays; Pt.2 British Seaside Holiday Resorts; Pt.3 A holiday environment; Pt.4 Holiday environments in W. Europe; Pt.5 Holidays and the travel industry; Pt.6 Seasonal nature of holidays; Pt.7 Tourism as big business
- **Unit 5 — The Future:** The future

**PEOPLE, PLACE AND WORK**

| | | | 1 | 2 | 3 | 4 | 5 | 6 | 7 | 8 | 9 |
|---|---|---|---|---|---|---|---|---|---|---|---|
| UNIT 1 | Why Work? | Pt.1 Work for what? | | | | | | | | | |
| | | Pt.2 People in and out of work | | | | | | | | | |
| | | Pt.3 Work and Leisure | | | | | | | | | |
| UNIT 2 | Patterns of Work | Pt.1 Places and work | > | | > | | | > | | | |
| | | Pt.2 Journey to work | > | | | | > | | | | |
| | | Pt.3 Occupational Structures - city, region - state | | | | | | | | | |
| UNIT 3 | Change in Work | Pt.1 Decline in employment | | | | > | | | | | |
| | | Pt.2 The changing countryside | | | | | > | | | | |
| | | Pt.3 Improved accessibility | | | | | | | | | |
| | | Pt.4 Environment and opportunity | | | | | | | | | |
| | | Pt.5 Energy for work | > | | | > | | | | | |
| | | Pt.6 Political intervention | | > | > | | > | | | | |
| | | Pt.7 Mobility of Labour | | > | | | | | | | |
| UNIT 4 | Change in Work | Pt.1 Washington - decline in local mining | > | | | | > | | | | |
| | | Pt.2 Washington Newtown - growth of new jobs | | > | | > | > | | > | | |
| UNIT 5 | Work and Environment | Pt.1 Work - environmental gain? | > | | | | | | | | > |
| | | Pt.2 Work - environmental disaster? | | | | | | | > | > | > |
| | | Pt.3 Changing perceptions and changing impact through time | > | | | | | | | | > |
| UNIT 6 | Work and the Future | Pt.1 Mass production - job satisfaction? | | > | | | | | | | |
| | | Pt.2 Work for Whom? | | > | | | > | | | | |
| | | Pt.3 Changing pattern of working life | | > | | | | | | | |

**CITIES AND PEOPLE**

| | | | 1 | 2 | 3 | 4 | 5 | 6 | 7 | 8 | 9 |
|---|---|---|---|---|---|---|---|---|---|---|---|
| UNIT 1 | Introduction | Pt.1 Urbanization | | | | | | | | | |
| | | Pt.2 World cities | | | | | | | | | |
| | | Pt.3 Nineteenth Century Urban Problems | | | | | | | | | |
| | | Pt.4 Images of a city | | | | | | | | | |
| UNIT 2 | City Environments | Pt.1 City Environments - inner city area / - inner city redevelopment / - suburbia / - outer city council estate | > | > | | | | | > | | |
| | | Pt.2 Local Residential Area | > | > | | | | | > | | |
| | | Pt.3 Patterns within cities | | | | | | | | | |
| | | Pt.4 Patterns within cities - land use | | | | | | | | | |
| | | Pt.5 Local town or city | > | | | > | | | | | |
| UNIT 3 People on the move in cities | Daily Rhythm | Pt.1 Individual movements within the community | > | | | | | | | | |
| | | Pt.2 The journey to work | | | | > | > | | | | |
| | | Pt.3 Movement for goods and services | > | | | | | | > | | |
| | | Pt.4 Urban transport systems | | | | > | | | | > | |
| | | Pt.5 Inter-city network | | | | > | | | > | | |
| UNIT 4 People on the move in cities | A place to live | Pt.1 Moving in and out of local area | | | > | | | | | | |
| | | Pt.2 Moving into cities | | | > | | | | | > | |
| | | Pt.3 Concentration within the city | | | | | > | | | | |
| | | Pt.4 Change within the city | | | | > | | | > | | |
| | | Pt.5 Moving out of cities | | | | > | | | | | |
| UNIT 5 Planning for cities | | Pt.1 Planning for the local area | > | | | > | | | | | |
| | | Pt.2 Planning for the region | > | | | > | | | | | |
| | | Community involvement | > | | | > | | | | | |
| UNIT 6 The Future in Britain | | Pt.1 Housing - what sort of provision | | | | | | | | > | |
| | | Pt.2 Scarcity of land - true or false | | | | | | | | > | |
| | | Pt.3 Transport - do we have a choice? | | | | | | | | > | |

# 4  TOPICS

**An excerpt from the syllabus, listing topics and indicating the local, national and world cover recommended:**

THEME 3 — PEOPLE, PLACE AND WORK (Contd.)

| TOPICS | LOCAL | NATIONAL | WORLD |
|---|---|---|---|
| UNIT 3 (contd.) | | | |
| 2. The Changing Countryside | Comparative studies with Ringmer and Kilham. | — Employment and Farming — Ringmer (Sussex), and Kilham (E. Riding) — changing socio-economic structure of the village. — Warrington — 'Crossover' near M6 and M62 intersection. — Central Birmingham. | |
| 3. Improved Accessibility | | | |
| 4. Environment and Opportunity | — Leisure/social environment as a location factor. | | |
| 5. Energy for Work. | — Environmental perception. | | Ghana — importance of Volta Power Scheme. — Stage of economic growth. E.E.C. — varying standards of living. Italy — Mezzogiorno. |
| 6. Political Intervention | | | China — labour organisation. W. Europe — distribution and origin of immigrant workers. France — housing immigrants. |
| 7. Mobility of Labour. | | | W. Europe — immigrants — the future. |

## THEME 3 — PEOPLE, PLACE AND WORK (Contd.)

| TOPICS | LOCAL | NATIONAL | WORLD |
|---|---|---|---|
| UNIT 4 — CHANGE IN WORK. | | | |
| 1. Decline of Coal Mining. | | — Nature of area (pre-development)<br>— Decline in mining.<br>— Consequences for the individual.<br>— Nature of area (post-development)<br>— Employment growth<br>— Consequences. | |
| 2. Growth of Jobs | | | |
| UNIT 5 — WORK AND ENVIRONMENT | | | |
| 1. Work — Environmental Gain? | | Man-made cf. 'natural' environments.<br>Fawley — oil refinery. | — gains/losses<br>— Arctic and Desert (U.S.S.R.)<br>Reclaimed land (Netherlands)<br>— Forest (New Zealand) |
| 2. Work — Environmental Disaster? | | Environmental problems —<br>e.g. London airport:<br>Flixborough.<br>— N. Kent — landscape of 1834 cf. present.<br>— Scotland — N. Sea Oil<br>— Drumbuie. | |

THEME 3 — PEOPLE, PLACE AND WORK (Contd.)

| TOPICS | LOCAL | NATIONAL | WORLD |
|---|---|---|---|
| **UNIT 5 (Contd.)** | | | |
| 3. Changing Perceptions and Changing Impact through Time. | Simulation: The Work and Environment Game.<br>— decisions and actions of one generation may change environment for succeeding generations. | | |
| **UNIT 6 — WORK AND THE FUTURE** | | | |
| 1. Mass production — Job Satisfaction? | | | Volvo (Sweden) — 'assembly line' — benefits for individuals. |
| 2. Work for Whom? | | Nationalization — Private Enterprise.<br>Mixed Economy. | |
| 3. Changing Pattern of Working Life. | — leisure time spent on household chores.<br>— School and work.<br>— Retirement. | | Multi-National Companies. International comparisons of women's working hours at home. |

## METHOD OF COURSE ASSESSMENT

1. *MARK ALLOCATION*

| | |
|---|---|
| Terminal Examination | 40% of total marks. |
| Individual Study | 20% of total marks. |
| Continuous Assessment | 40% of total marks. |

2. *LEVELS OF UNDERSTANDING*

In the final assessment, marks will be awarded for specific abilities based very broadly on Bloom's 'Taxonomy of Educational Objectives':

a) Knowledge (Recall)

— the pupil's ability to store information in his mind and recall it later in substantially the same form. This may include knowledge of terms, facts, rules and principles.

b) Comprehension

— the pupil's ability to understand information which is supplied. This may include, for example, the ability to interpret data, to draw inferences and conclusions from data, and to predict trends.

c) Application

— the pupil's ability to use his knowledge and comprehension of a subject to solve a problem which is new to him.

d) Judgement

— the pupil's ability to make judgements concerning for example the value of various solutions to a problem or methods of tackling a problem.

The weighting of the mark allocation will be approximately:—

| | | |
|---|---|---|
| Knowledge (Recall) | — | 30% |
| Comprehension | — | 40% |
| Application/Judgment | — | 30% |

Wherever possible, it is intended that this weighting should apply to internal test items that form part of the Continuous Assessment element.

3. *TERMINAL EXAMINATION*

One paper of 1³/₄ hours duration plus 15 mins. reading time.
The paper will be divided into three sections:—

| | |
|---|---|
| Section A | Man, Land and Leisure. |
| Section B | Cities and People. |
| Section C | People, Place and Work. |

Questions will be of a data response type, There will be three questions set in each section, and candidates will be required to attempt FOUR questions, ONE from each section and ONE other. Each question will carry 10% of the total marks.

## 4. *INDIVIDUAL STUDY*

This study is to be completed by the half term of the Spring Term prior to the terminal examination. It should be related to some aspect of the syllabus themes and must be based on the candidate's field work – either in the local area or further afield, although obviously relevant supporting secondary source material should be used.

a) *Pupil guidelines*

A candidate should be aiming at a study with:

1) A clearly defined question or problem suitable for geographical analysis.
2) A clear structure, showing a local development of geographical enquiry including a clear conclusion.
3) Adequate, accurate and relevant use of primary and secondary sources of information.
4) A high standard of graphicacy (i.e. maps, diagrams, and illustrations that are well produced and linked to the written text).
5) A high standard of written communication (i.e. quality of writing, spelling and clarity of expression).

b) *Mark Allocation*

In view of the above, the following marking allocation is suggested:—

| | |
|---|---|
| 1) Geographical problem/question | 4 marks |
| 2) Structure | 4 marks |
| 3) Use of primary & secondary sources | 4 marks |
| 4) Graphicacy | 4 marks |
| 5) Literacy | 4 marks |
| Total | 20 marks |

It is suggested that each assessment criterion should be graded on the following scale:

| | |
|---|---|
| Very good | 4 marks |
| Good | 3 marks |
| Satisfactory | 2 marks |

Weak                    1 mark
Unsatisfactory          0 marks

There is no specific mark allocation for 'initiative and originality' as it is suggested that these qualities will be taken into account by the assessor under several different criteria headings — e.g. 'problem', 'use of data', 'methods of presentation' etc.

*Note:*

a) Whilst it is difficult to lay down specific guidelines for the amount of time to be spent on this element, a time equivalent of one term's work over two years might be suggested.

## 5. CONTINUOUS ASSESSMENT

This element carries 40% of the total marks and this will be shared amongst three units:—

i) The first unit will consist of five test items set and be administered internally by each school. Each test item will carry 5% of the total marks, giving a sub-total of 25% of the total marks for this unit.

ii) The second unit will consist of an O.S. map test item, set centrally but administered internally, carrying 5% of the total marks.

iii) The third unit will consist of teacher assessment, and will carry 10% of the total marks.

## 6. DETAILS OF CONTINUOUS ASSESSMENT ELEMENTS

*i) Internal Test Items:*

No upper limit is set on the number of internal test items that may be given, but a minimum number of five sets of marks should be submitted or the candidate will forfeit 5% of the total marks for each set missing. Where more than five test items are conducted over the two years the best five results should be submitted to count towards the result of the examination. These tests are seen as integral to the course and whilst it is felt unnecessary to stipulate that they are administered under exam conditions they should reflect the pupils' ability to cope unaided by the teacher and should be of 30 to 35 mins. duration. It is also intended that in drawing up the test items, teacher's should attempt a balance of marks for Knowledge, Comprehension, Application/Judgment as set out in this syllabus. A sample internal test item, and sample record sheet for this unit are included in the Appendix.

*ii) O.S. Map Test Item*

This will be set centrally and test packs consisting of sets of maps and sets of question papers will be made available to schools. The assessment of this unit will be made in Terms 4 or 5 of the course and will be of 30 to 35 mins. duration. A sample map question is included in the Appendix.

*iii) Teacher Assessment*

This unit is intended to allow the teacher to give credit for what is considered to be an important aspect of the course – pupil motivation/participation. The final mark for this unit will derive from termly grades based on the following criteria:—

  a) Attendance
  b) Perseverance
  c) Responsiveness
  d) Imagination
  e) Responsibility

Each criterion should be graded on the following scale:—

| | |
|---|---|
| Very Good | 4 marks |
| Good | 3 marks |
| Satisfactory | 2 marks |
| Weak | 1 mark |
| Unsatisfactory | 0 marks |

A sample record sheet is included in the Appendix.

7. *SUMMARY OF MARK ALLOCATION*

|  |  |  |  |
|---|---|---|---|
| i) Final Examination | | | 40% |
| ii) Project | | | 20% |
| iii) Continuous Assessment: | | | |
|  a) Internal Test Items | 25% | | |
|  b) O.S. Map Test Item | 5% | | |
|  c) Teacher Assessment | 10% | 40% | |
|  | | 100% | |

Sample Summary Sheets for:

  a) Continuous Assessment Element
  b) Complete Assessment

are included in the Appendix.

# Appendix C to Chapter Seven
University of Sussex, Centre for Educational Technology.
Volkswagen Curriculum Analysis Project

## SCHEME FOR THE ANALYSIS OF CURRICULUM MATERIALS*

*PART 1.*    *INTRODUCTION*
1.1 Basic Facts
1.2 Author's Rationale
1.3 Issues and Perspectives

*PART 2.*    *DESCRIPTION AND ANALYSIS OF THE MATERIALS*
2.1 Description of Pupil Materials
2.2 Description of Teacher Materials
2.3 Structure of the Materials

*PART 3.*    *THE MATERIALS IN USE*
3.1 Main Features
3.2 Possible Modifications and Additions
3.3 Patterns of Use
3.4 Implications for Implementation

*PART 4.*    *EVALUATION*
4.1 Other Sources of Evidence
4.2 Evaluation of Aims
4.3 Evaluation of Curriculum Strategy
4.4 Evaluation of Materials
4.5 Suitability for the Context

*PART 5.*    *DECISION MAKING IN A SPECIFIC CONTEXT*
(Optional)
5.1 Constraints of the Particular Context
5.2 Possible Patterns of Use
5.3 Implementation Strategies
5.4 Summary of Decision Issues

*This scheme is reproduced with permission from M. Eraut, L. Goad and G. Smith (1975), *The Analysis of Curriculum Materials*, University of Sussex Education Area, which also includes advice on how to use the scheme.

## PART 1. INTRODUCTION
1.1   Basic Facts

    1.1.1   State briefly the author(s), Title(s), date(s), publisher and price(s). Where the material consists of more than one physical resource, (e.g. a book, a tape, a set of slides or a pack of worksheets), list each one separately and indicate its size in terms of number of pages, number of items, minutes of running time, etc. Also state whether the resource is primarily intended for pupil use or teacher use.

    1.1.2   What does the material, in its own terms, state to be its aim and function?

    1.1.3   State briefly the target audience and situation; e.g. pupil's age, interests and ability range, examination orientation, type of school and course duration.

    1.1.4   What provision, if any, was made for testing the material in draft form and revising it prior to publication?

    1.1.5   If it is helpful, prepare an informative appendix on the author(s)' credentials and background. Include any other relevant publications; and, where an official project is concerned, its early history and original brief.

1.2   Author's Rationale
Summarise any explanation or justification for the materials provided by the author, either in the materials under analysis or, if particularly relevant, in other publications.

1.3   Issues and Perspectives
Indicate the main issues raised by the analysis.

## PART 2. DESCRIPTION AND ANALYSIS OF THE MATERIALS
2.1   Description of Pupil Materials

    2.1.1   Describe the content of the material, using any of the techniques listed below that seem appropriate.

    *Overview*
Listing major topics; titles or groups of chapters; chapter headings; sub-chapter arrangement; recurring themes; topics listed in the index.

    *Detail*
Sampling the material by selecting typical or important sections and describing their contents at a detailed level. Indicating in quantitative terms the relative emphasis given to different aspects of the subject matter.

2.1.2   Describe the presentation of the material and relate it to the various categories of content.

2.1.3   Describe the pupil exercises or tasks that are included in the material; and indicate how frequently each type of task occurs and how the tasks are sequenced and/or repeated.

2.1.4   List any explicit statements on pupil assessment; and note examples of tests or assessment schemes (indicating both the nature of any specific instruments and the structure of the assessment pattern as a whole).

2.1.5   List, summarise or describe any statements of purpose, aim or objectives included in the pupil material.

2.1.6   List and estimate the frequency and significance of directions to the pupil to refer to his teacher or to use special facilities.

2.1.7   Where there is more than one physical resource, indicate the inter-relationships between them in terms of cross-referencing, sequencing and repetition, both of content and of pupil tasks.

2.2   Description of the Teacher Materials

2.2.1   Indicate where material for the teacher is to be found, and describe the content of the teacher's materials as a whole using any of the techniques listed under 2.1.1 that seem appropriate.

2.2.2   Describe the presentation form of the material.

2.2.3   Describe any additional pupil roles or tasks that are mentioned or included; and indicate the frequency and sequencing.

2.2.4   List any explicit statements on pupil assessment; and note examples of tests or assessment schemes (indicating both the nature of any specific assessment instruments and the structure of the assessment pattern as a whole).

2.2.5   List, summarise or describe any statements of purpose, aim or objectives that are included in the teacher's material; and indicate whether they refer to learning by (a) the pupil or (b) the teacher.

2.2.6   Describe the teacher tasks and roles that are stated in the materials; and indicate the extent of their demands on the teacher's time.

2.2.7 List any statements about the need for further resources or special facilities.

2.3 Structure of the Materials

2.3.1 How do pupil materials and teacher materials fit together and are there any obvious points of conflict?

2.3.2 Describe the coverage of the subject matter in terms of knowledge, skills and attitudes To what extent is the material explicitly concerned with the presentation of values or the development of attitudes?

2.3.3 Indicate the generality and the level of abstraction of the subject matter. Does it mainly consist of factual material or does it try to communicate specific concepts, general concepts or principles? What are the roles of illustrations, applications and examples? What kinds of argument are used and how much supporting evidence is given? Does it develop specific techniques or general patterns of behaviour?

2.3.4 What pre-requisite knowledge and skills are needed by the pupil?

2.3.5 How is the subject matter organised in terms of structure, sequence or cumulative build-up; and how do the pupil tasks change?

2.3.6 What image of the subject matter is most likely to be communicated? What are its boundaries and what are its chief concerns? What implicit values can be detected in the selection or interpretation of information?

2.3.7 How do pupil tasks and teacher activities relate to each other and how do they vary with the subject matter?

2.3.8 How is the assessment related to pupil tasks (congruency?) and to the subject matter (uniformity of emphasis?)

2.3.9 Where and if there are stated objectives how do these relate to pupil tasks and to the assessment pattern?

## PART 3. THE MATERIALS IN USE

3.1 Main Features

Summarise the main features of the materials and the recommended pattern of use, indicating which curriculum decisions would be pre-empted by the decision to adopt the materials and which would still be the responsibility of the user group.

The authors have found a curriculum model especially useful for bringing out the main features and their inter-relationships; and this approach is outlined in the Introduction and Guide. It is not built into the scheme because some authorities prefer to operate without such a model.

3.2　Possible Modifications and Additions

Describe ways in which the materials or the recommended patterns of use may be modified or supplemented when implementing a curriculum based on them. Indicate where there is no scope for alteration within the term of the overall curriculum strategy, and note how much further curriculum planning is likely to be necessary.

3.3　Patterns of Use

Describe some possible patterns of use in the context of the overall school curriculum. Which pupils are involved and when? How does it relate to areas of the curriculum which come before it and after it? What, if any, modifications and additions are to be incorporated? What, if any, form of assessment is intended?

3.4　Implications for Implementation

3.4.1　How much teacher time is needed *prior* to implementation for activities such as gaining familiarity with the curriculum, further planning, and selecting or producing further materials?

3.4.2　How much of his time and energy is likely to be committed
a) in the first year b) subsequently?

3.4.3　What are the implications for the school in terms of teacher provision, in-service training, special facilities and finance?

3.4.4　Discuss the implications for the pupil with reference to subject selection, examination focus and future employment.

3.4.5　What knowledge, skills and attitudes are demanded of the teacher?

3.4.6　Discuss the implications for the school in terms of school aims and the articulation of this curriculum area with those preceding, accompanying or following it.

3.4.7　Discuss the implications for the school district and the community in terms of attitudes, provision of in-service training and special facilities and finance.

3.4.8 What major problems are likely to result from implementation in probable *non-ideal* situations?


## PART 4. EVALUATION

4.1 Other Sources of Evidence

    4.1.1 The development of the resource

        (i) What evidence of developmental testing is available? (i.e. testing that is primarily intended to show how the resource can be improved).

        (ii) Is there evidence that improvements resulted from the development phase?

    4.1.2 Validation

        (i) What reports are available from the author, publisher or independent evaluator?

        (ii) Was the evaluation qualitative or quantitative?

        (iii) What was the evidence of final validation?

    4.1.3 What information about the users of the resource and their experience is available?

    4.1.4 Where has the resource been reviewed and what were the major evaluative comments?

    4.1.5 What unintended outcomes or side-effects have been reported?

    4.1.6 Is there any evaluative evidence from comparable and similar resources?

    4.1.7 The analyst is invited to comment on the evaluation evidence available in terms of its relevance to users supporting differing aims and strategies.

4.2 Give arguments for and against pursuing the particular aims endorsed by the materials in this area of the curriculum. Relate your arguments to potentially competing aims, the patterns of use outlined in Part 3 and various forms of traditional practice.

4.3 Give arguments for and against the particular curriculum strategy assumed or advocated for achieving these aims, again relating your arguments to potentially competing strategies, the patterns of use outlined in Part 3 and various forms of traditional practice.

4.4 Evaluate the materials and their adequacy for supporting the aims and curriculum strategy.

4.5   Giving special attention to patterns of use (3.3) and implementation problems (3.4), evaluate the feasibility of using the materials in various contexts.


# Appendix D to Chapter Seven

## READABILITY INDICES

### 1. The Rudolph Flesch Formula

The original Rudolph Flesch Formula (1943) has undergone numerous revisions and refinements by Flesch and others. Basically, it comprises two measures, those of Reading Ease and Human Interest. The instructions for the use of Flesch's 1948 revision of the Reading Ease Formula are as follows:

To measure the readability of a passage, the following steps must be taken:

Systematically select 100 word samples from the text.
Determine the number of syllables per 100 words.
Determine the average number of words per sentence.

These factors are represented by wl (word length) and sl (sentence length) respectively in the formula given.

Calculate the following equation:

Reading Ease = 206.835 − .846wl − 1.015sl.

Reading Ease represents the Grade Level which would have to be attained in order to read the passage.

To determine the Human Interest Level of written material, these instructions are followed.

Select 100 word samples as above.
Count the number of personal words per 100 words (pw).
Count the number of personal sentences per 100 sentences (ps).

Calculate the equation:

Human Interest = 3.635pw − .314ps.

When applying the Flesch Formulae, sampling is left to the discretion of the user, not only in terms of where to make the selection, but also in terms of the number of samples required throughout particular material.

## 2. ASEP Modification To Flesch

One modification of the Flesch Formulae was used by the developer of the Australian Science Education Project, 1970, and this modification provides explicit directives for the selection of samples. (Adapted from ASEP Mimeograph, October, 1970).

Selecting Samples:

1. 3−5 in an article.
2. 25−30 in a book.
3. Make a random selection, e.g. every third paragraph, every other page.
4. Don't use introductory paragraphs.
5. Start each sample at the beginning of a paragraph.

The calculation of the Reading Ease equation given earlier provides for a quantitative assessment of the raw score in terms of a Grade equivalent. A qualitative assessment of the score of average sentence length and the number of syllables per 100 words can be gained from the table overleaf.

| Reading Ease Score | Description of Style | Typical Magazine | Grade Equivalent |
|---|---|---|---|
| 90−100 | Very Easy | Comics | 5th |
| 80−90 | Easy | Pulp Fiction | 6th |
| 70−80 | Fairly Easy | Slick Fiction | 7th |
| 60−70 | Standard | Digests, *Time* | 8th−9th |
| 50−60 | Fairly Difficult | *Harper's, Atlantic* | 10th−12th |
| 30−50 | Difficult | Academic | 13th−16th |
| 0−30 | Very Difficult | Scientific | College |

Similarly, the Human Interest score may be qualitatively interpreted by reference to a Table.

| Human Interest Score (Recorded as Percentage of Personal Words and Personal Sentences) | Description of Style | Typical Magazine |
|---|---|---|
| 60−100 | Dramatic | Fiction |
| 40−60 | Highly Interesting | *New Yorker* |
| 20−40 | Interesting | Digests, *Time* |
| 10−20 | Mildly Interesting | Trade |
| 0−10 | Dull | Scientific, Professional |

### 3. Gunning's Fog Index

Gunning's Fog Index (1952) uses a word and sentence count to determine a Grade Level of Difficulty of written material. The formula, which is applied to systematically selected 100 word passages from a text, is simple.

Grade Level = .4 (average sentence length over 100 words + the number of three or more syllable words throughout the passage.)

Based on the same factors as the Flesch Formula for Reading Ease, the Fog Index limits the syllable count to 'hard' words which are those of three or more syllables, thus taking less time to administer.

The measure is largely that of reading ease in terms of reading rate (influenced by the incidence of 'hard' or polysyllabic words), and memory span (influenced by sentence length).

# References

Adams, A. (1976). *The Humanities Jungle*, Ward Lock Educational.

Bailey, P. (1974). *Teaching Geography*, David and Charles.

Barrow, R. (1976). *Common Sense and the Curriculum*, Allen and Unwin.

Bates, A. W. (1973). 'The Planning of the Curriculum', in Fowler, G., Morris, V., Ozga, J. (Ed.), *Decision Making in British Education*, Heinemann and Open University.

Bee, (Bulletin of Environmental Education) May 1975, Number 49, GYSL Special Issue, Town and Country Planning Association.

Benjamin, H. (1939). 'The Saber-tooth curriculum', in Hooper, R. (Ed.), (1971), *The Curriculum: context, design and development*, Olivers and Boyd.

Beswick, N. (1976). *Organizing Resources*, Heinemann.

Biddle, D. S. and Shortle, D. (1969). *Programme Planning in Geography*, Martindale Press (Australia).

Biddle, D. S. (1974). *An Investigation into the Use of Curriculum Theory in the Formation of a Systems Model for the Construction and Evaluation of Secondary School Curricula in England and Wales*, unpublished Ph.D. Thesis, University of London.

Biddle, D. S. (in press). 'Course Planning in Geography' in Graves, N. J. (Ed.), *New Unesco Sourcebook for Geography Teaching*, Unesco.

Biddle, D. S. (1976). 'Paradigms in Geography; some implications for curriculum development', *Geographical Education*, vol. 2, no. 4, 1976.

Bloom, B. S. *et al* (1956). *Taxonomy of educational objectives — The cognitive domain*, Longmans.

Blyth, A. W., Cooper, K., Derricott, R., Elliot, G., Sumner, H., Waplington, A. (1976). *Curriculum Planning in History, Geography and Social Science*, Collins — E.S.L.

Bobbitt, F. (1918). *The curriculum*, Houghton Mifflin.

Bobbitt, F. (1924). *How to make a curriculum*, Houghton Mifflin.

Briault, E. W. H. and Shave, D. W. (1952). *Geography in Secondary Schools with Special Reference to the Secondary Modern School*, Geography Association.

Broek, J. O. M. (1965). *Geography, its scope and spirit*, Charles E. Merrill Books Inc.

Bruce, G. (1969). *Secondary School Examinations, Facts and Commentary*, Pergamon.

Burtonwood, N. (1976). 'A concept-based course for geography for the 4th and 5th year', *Classroom Geographer*, April 1976.

Chorley, R. J. and Haggett, P. (Ed.), (1965) (1970). *Frontiers in Geographical Teaching*, Methuen.

Clark, M. J., Ricketts, P. J. (1976). 'Barton does not rule the waves', *The Geographical Magazine*, vol. 48, no. 10.

Committee of Enquiry into the Management and Government of Schools (Taylor Report), *A new partnership for our schools*, HMSO, 1977.

Cromarty, D. (1975). 'Reconstructing the syllabus', *Teaching Geography*, vol. 1, no. 1, April 1975.

Crowther, G. (1959). *15–18 Report of the Central Advisory Council for Education in England*, vol. 1, H.M.S.O.

Davies, R. L. (1976) *Marketing Geography*, Methuen.

Department of Education and Science (1977a). *Educating our children*, H.M.S.O.

Department of Education and Science (1977b). *Education in schools: a consultative document*, H.M.S.O.

Department of Education and Science (1978). *The teaching of ideas in geography: some suggestions for the middle and secondary years of education.* H.M.S.O.

Education Department (1975) *Geography Course Construction Rationale*, Glenbervie Teachers Centre, Victoria, Australia.

Elliott, G. and Saunders, M. (1976). 'Project and School Working Together', in Boden, P., *Developments in Geography Teaching*, Open Books.

Fairgrieve, J. (1926). *Geography in School*, U.L.P.

Fenton, E. (Ed.) (1966), *The New Social Studies in Secondary Schools*, Holt, Rinehart and Winston.

Frey, A. (1978). 'The N and F proposals: Geography in the next decade? *Teaching Geography*, vol. 3, no. 3, January 1978.

Gelsthorpe, T. (1976). 'Beyond the Curriculum Package', in Boden, P., *Developments in Geography Teaching*, Open Books.

Ghaye, A. L. (1977). 'A syllabus for geography in the lower school', *Classroom Geographer*, January 1977.

Graves, N. J. (1968). 'An investigation into the teaching of Asia in English and Welsh secondary schools', in I.G.U. Abstract and papers edited by S. Das Gupta and T. Romanonska, Lakshmman (Calcutta).

Graves, N. J. (1971). *Geography in Secondary Education*, Geographical Association.

Graves, N. J. (1977). *Geography in Education*, Heinemann.

Graves, N. J., White, J. T. (1976). *Geography of the British Isles*, Heinemann.

Graves, N. J. (1977). 'Geography and the N and F examination proposals, *Teaching Geography*, vol. 2, no. 3, January 1977.

Grenyer, N. (1978). 'A common syllabus for N and F levels? *Teaching Geography*, vol. 3, no. 3, January 1978.

Gronlund, N. E. (1970). *Stating Behavioural Objectives for Classroom Instruction*, Collier, Macmillan.

Haggett, P. (1972, 1975). *Geography a Modern Synthesis*, Harper and Row.
Hall, D. (1976). *Geography and the geography teacher*, Allen and Unwin.
Hamilton, D. (1976). *Curriculum Evaluation*, Open Books.
Hamilton, D., Jenkins, D., King, C., MacDonald, B., Parlett, M. (Ed.) (1977). *Beyond the numbers game*, Macmillan.
Hickman, G., Reynolds, J. and Tolley, H. (1973). *A New Professionalism for a Changing Geography*, Schools Council.
Hill, W. (Ed.) (1963). *Curriculum Guide for Geographic Education*, National Council for Geographic Education (U.S.A.).
Hogan, M. M. (1962). *The Evolution of the Regional Concept and its Influence on the Teaching of Geography in School*, unpublished M.A. thesis, University of London.

I.A.A.M. (1967). *The Teaching of Geography in Secondary Schools*, C.U.P.

James, E. (1949). *An Essay on the Content of Education*, Harrap.

Kemp, J. E. (1971). *Instructional Design*, Fearon.
Kerr, J. F. (Ed.) (1968) *Changing the Curriculum*, U.L.P.
Kohn, C. F. (in press). 'Solving Real Problems in Geographical Education', in Graves, N. J. (Ed.), *New Unesco Source Book for Geography Teaching*.
Krathwohl, D. R. *et al.* (1964). *Taxonomy of educational objectives. The affective domain*, Longman.

Lawton, D. (1973). *Social Change, Educational Theory and Curriculum Planning*, U.L.P.
Lawton, D. (1975). *Class Culture and the Curriculum*, R.K.P.
Lawton, D. (1977). *Education and Social Justice*, Sage.
Lawton, D., Dufour, B. (1973). *The New Social Studies*, Heinemann.
Ley, D. (1977). 'Social Geography and the taken-for-granted world', *Transactions of the Institute of British Geographers New Series*, vol. 2, no. 4.
Lidstone, J. G. (1977). *An evaluation of the geography curriculum offered to second and third year pupils in a small London junior high school*, based on volumes 2 and 3 of the *Oxford Geography Project* text books, unpublished M.A. dissertation, University of London.
Long, M. (ed.) (1974). *Handbook for Geography Teachers*, Methuen.
Long, M. and Robertson, B. S. (1966). *Teaching Geography*, Heinemann.

MacDonald, B. and Walker, R. (1976). *Changing the Curriculum*, Open Books.
Mager, R. F. (1962). *Preparing Instructional Objectives*, Fearon.
Marsden, W. E. (1976). *Evaluating the geography curriculum*, Oliver and Boyd.
Marsden, W. D. (1976a). 'Principles, Concepts and Exemplars, and the structuring of Curriculum Units in Geography', *Geographical Education*, vol. 2, 1976.

Naish, M. C. (1976). 'Geography 16–19, A New Schools Council Curriculum Development Project', *Teaching Geography*, vol. 1, no. 3.

Naish, M. C. (1978). 'Progress and Planning in the Geography 16–19 Project', *Classroom Geographer*, January 1978.

Oliver, D. W. (1966). 'The Selection of Content in the Social Sciences', in Fenton, E. *Teaching the New Social Studies in Secondary Schools*, Holt, Rinehart and Winston.

Owen, J. G. (1973). *The Management of Curriculum Development*, C.U.P.

Peters, R. S. (1965). 'What is an education process?' in Peters, R. S. (Ed.) *The Concept of Education*, R.K.P.

Peters, R. S. (1966). *Ethics and Education*, Allen and Unwin.

Popham, W. J. (1969). 'Objectives and instruction', in Popham, W. J., Eisner, E. W., Sullivan, H. J. and Tyler, L. C. *Instructional Objectives*, American Educational Research Association, Monograph Series on Curriculum Evaluation, N. J. Rand, McNally.

Pring, R. (1976). *Knowledge and Schooling*, Open Books.

Reynolds, J. and Skilbeck, M. (1976). *Culture and the Classroom*, Open Books.

Rosenthal, R., Jacobson, L. (1968). *Pygmalion in the Classroom*, Holt, Rinehart and Winston.

Schon, D. (1971). *Beyond the Stable State*, Temple Smith.

Schools Council (1972). *Working Paper 43, School Resource Centres*, Evans/Methuen.

Schools Council (1972). *Working Paper 45, 16–19 Growth and Response, 1. Curricular Bases*, Evans/Methuen.

Schools Council (1973a). *Working Paper 46, 16–19 Growth and Response, 2. Examination Structure*, Evans/Methuen.

Schools Council (1973b). *Working Paper 47, Preparing for Degree Courses*, Evans/Methuen.

Schools Council (1974/75). *Geography for the Young School Leaver Project: Man, Land and Leisure; Cities and Peoples; People, Place and Work*, Nelson.

Schools Council (1977a). *Towards N and F: A Modular Curriculum*, Teaching Research Unit, Curriculum and Methods Department, Faculty of Education, University of Birmingham.

Schools Council (1977b). *Report of the Geography Syllabus Steering Group to the Joint Examinations Sub-Committee of the Schools Council*, School Government Publishing Co.

Schools Council (1978a). Examinations Bulletin 38 – Examination at 18+, Evans/Methuen.

Schools Council (1978). *Geography 14–18 Project: Classroom Units on Industry, Transport Networks, Population, Urban Geography*, Macmillan.

Small, R. J. (1969). 'The New Geomorphology and the Sixth Former', *Geography*, vol. 54, 1967.

Sockett, H. (1976). *Designing the Curriculum*, Open Books.

South Australian Education Dept. (1978). *Objectives in Junior Secondary Geography*, Government Printer, South Australia.

Stenhouse, L. (1975). *An Introduction to Curriculum Research and Development*, Heinemann.

Taba, H. (1962). *Curriculum Development: Theory and Practice*, Harcourt, Brace and World.

Tanner, D. and Tanner, L. N. (1975). *Curriculum Development: Theory into Practice*, Collier Macmillan.

Taylor Report (1977). See Committee of Enquiry into the Management and Government of Schools.

Taylor, P. K., Reid, W. A., Holley, B. J. (1974). *The English Sixth Form: A Case Study in Curriculum Research*, Routledge and Kegan Paul.

*Teachers Talking about the GYSL Project*, vol. 3, Autumn 1976, Nelson.

Tolley, H., Reynolds, J. B. (1977). *Geography 14–18: A Handbook for School-based Curriculum Development*, Macmillan.

Tumman, L. (1977). *The Avery Hill 14–16 Project*, GYSL, ILEA Geography Bulletin No. 1, November 1977.

Tyler, R. W. (1949). *Basic Principles of Curriculum and Instruction*, University of Chicago Press.

University of London (1978). *General Certificate of Education Examination, Regulations and Syllabuses*.

Walker, M. J. (1976). 'Changing the Curriculum', *Teaching Geography*, vol. 1, no. 4, April, 1976.

Warwick, D. (1975). *Curriculum Structure and Design*, U.L.P.

West Midlands Geography Teachers' Group (1974). *Advanced Level Geography Syllabus, University of Birmingham and Joint Matriculation Board: Joint Project for Advanced Level Syllabuses and Examinations*.

Wheatley, A. (1976). 'Implementing a Resource Based Project', in Boden, P., *Developments in Geography Teaching*, Open Books.

Wheeler, D. K. (1967). *Curriculum Process*, U.L.P.

# General Index

*To avoid confusion over classification of pupils the index has adopted age groups; thus a programme suitable for 15 year-old will be found under 15 within the entry "age groups".*

*Attention is drawn to the Author Index which follows the General Index which should be considered in conjunction with the Bibliography Title given in the Authorship Table on pp. 169–73.*